THINGS TO DO IN A DAY

Macmillan Publishing Co., Inc.
New York

Credits
Designers: Harry Butler 26, 28, 40, 58
David Bailie 30
Ron Kidd 14, 22, 32, 38, 42
Alf Martensson 12, 16, 24, 36, 44, 52, 56, 62
R. Smith 48
Goodwin Sorrell 8
L. Vernon 54
Suppliers: Transletters Ltd (Transfers) 8
Selfridges Ltd (toys) 8
Habitat (crockery and cutlery) 16
John Lewis Ltd (crockery and cutlery) 20
(cushion) 24, (coffee set, cushions, maize
matting) 26, (umbrellas) 42, (kitchen utensils)
54
Grundig (transistor radio) 22
Heals (rug and glass bowl) 22, (lamp, binders,
letter rack and stacking trays) 62
Butterfly Boutique, Beak Street, London
(clogs) 24, (garments) 40

Part of this material was first published by
Marshall Cavendish Limited in *Golden Homes*.

Macmillan Publishing Co., Inc.
866 Third Avenue, New York, N.Y. 10022

Library of Congress Cataloging in Publication Data
Main entry under title:
Things to do in a day.
    London ed. (M. Cavendish Publications) has title:
The do-it-yourself book of things to do in a day.
    1. Handicraft.
TT157.T48 1976   745.5   76-2035
ISBN 0-02-578240-1

First American Edition 1976

Printed in Great Britain

INTRODUCTION

Very few people have unlimited time at their disposal to spend on complicated do-it-yourself projects. On the other hand, everyone has the odd 'rainy day' or 'weekend with nothing to do'. As you look through these idea-filled chapters, you'll be delighted at the variety of things that you can make in just one day. Planned by experts, these specially organized projects give you maximum results for a minimum of time, with a really professional look into the bargain.

You'll find such useful items as storage boxes, tables, a fun bookcase for the children's room, a stylish magazine rack, a decorative spice rack, a colorful stool which can also be used as a table, and many other bright ideas, each with a distinctive design of its own, avoiding the mass-produced look and giving your home a unique personal touch. Having something to show for a day's work gives you an enormous sense of satisfaction. Why not start planning now for those free days later on?

Everything in *Things to do in a Day* is easy to make, and everyone will be tempted to try their hand. Clear step-by-step instructions, well-organized diagrams and superb color illustrations of the finished products are all you need to get results, and at the same time you are provided with an invaluable practical grounding in carpentry techniques. We have also provided a guide to the basic tools you'll need and a full explanation of their use. However you use this book, whether you're a beginner who wants to start out on a practical basis, or whether you're more proficient, but would welcome some new ideas for quick-to-make pieces, you'll be delighted with this special selection of things to do in a day.

CONTENTS

DATA SHEET

Carpenter's basic tool kit

NELSON HARGREAVES

There is a vast range of tools on the market for do-it-yourself jobs. Many of these have very specific uses. A collection of basic tools is, however, quite sufficient for most requirements. This DATA SHEET presents a basic tool kit for the home carpenter.

1. Tenon or back saw. These saws are available in blade lengths of between 8in and 14in (203mm and 355mm) with 13, 14, 15, 16 or 20 teeth per inch. This is used for jointing and cutting across the grain on small pieces. The back of the blade may be of brass or steel. The saw with 20 teeth per inch is for cutting dovetails and it has a thin blade to give greater accuracy. The dovetail saw performs a ripping action, so cut along the grain when using it.

2. Handsaw. This is used for cutting larger pieces of lumber. There are three types of handsaw. The one shown here is a panel saw. It is 20in to 22in (508mm to 558mm) long with 10 teeth per inch. Its special purpose is for fine crosscut and jointing work and for cutting plywood, blockboard and hardboard. The other types of handsaw (not shown) are the rip saw and the crosscut saw. The rip saw is 26in (661mm) long and 5 teeth per inch. Its special purpose is for cutting softwoods, working with the grain. The crosscut saw is 24in to 26in (610mm to 661mm) long with 6 to 8 teeth per inch and is used for cutting across the grain of hardwoods and softwoods and for working with the grain on very hard woods.

3. C clamps. These are used for a range of clamping purposes. These clamps are available in a 1in to 18in (25mm to 457mm) range of opening and between 1in to 8in (25mm to 203mm) depth of throat. When using C clamps always place a waste scrap of lumber between the piece to be clamped and the jaws of the clamps. This prevents bruising of the piece.

4. Ratchet brace. This has spring-loaded jaws in a screw-tightened chuck. It is specially designed for holding wood auger bits (5). The brace is available with or without a reversible

ratchet in a sweep (the arc described by the turning handle of the brace) ranging from 5⅞in (148mm) to 14in (355mm).

5. Wood auger bits. These are used with 4.

6. Hand drill. This is used for holding wood and metal twist drill bits (7) and countersink or rose bits (8). The example shown here has a double pinion (cogged drive wheel).

7. Twist bits. These are commonly available in sizes ranging from 1/64th to ½in (13mm). The type of steel used depends on the use to which the bit is to be put.

8. Rose countersink or reamer bit. This is used for countersinking drilled holes so that countersunk screwheads will fit flush with the surface of the piece you are working with.

9. Warrington pattern or cross peen hammer. This is used for general nailing and joinery and can be used for planishing and beating metal. Weights of these hammers range from 6oz (170g) to 16oz (450g).

10. Claw hammer. This is used for general purpose carpentry, in particular for driving and removing nails. When taking out nails, make sure that the nailhead is well into the claw of the hammer and, if it is necessary to protect the surface of the wood, place a scrap piece of lumber between the claw and the wood. Exert even pressure to lever the nail out. Claw hammers are available in weights ranging from 16oz (450g) to 24oz (570g).

11. Carpenter's or joiner's mallet. This is used for general carpentry and cabinet work and is available in head lengths of between 4in (100m) and 5½in (180mm).

12. Handyman's knife. This useful carpentry knife can be fitted with a variety of blades to suit specific purposes. The blades include angled concave, convex, linoleum and hooked blades. Wood and metal saw blades (**12A** and **12B**) can also be fitted to this tool as can a blade for cutting plastic laminate.

13. Bench plane. There are various types of bench plane and they are available in a range of lengths and widths. The smooth plane (shown here) comes in lengths of between 9½in and 10¼in (241mm to 260mm) and widths of between 1¾in and 2⅜in (44mm to 60mm). The Jack plane (not shown) is available in lengths of between 14in (356mm) and 15in (381mm) and widths ranging from 2in (50mm) to 2⅜in (60mm). The Fore plane (not shown) is 18in (457mm) long and 2⅜in (60mm) wide. The Jointer plane (not shown) is 22in (561mm) long and 2⅜in (60mm) wide. When working with resinous or sticky woods, a plane with a longitudinally corrugated sole makes the job of planing easier because friction between the lumber and the plane is reduced. If you do not have such a plane, apply a drop of vegetable oil to the sole of your ordinary plane — this will perform much the same function.

14. Surform plane. This is one of a range of open rasp/planing tools, all of which are useful and versatile. They are primarily used for rough work but with care some reasonably fine craftmanship can be produced. Each tool in this range has replaceable blades.

15. Block plane. This small plane is particularly useful for fine cabinet work and for planing end grain. Available in lengths of between 6in and 7in (152mm to 178mm) and cutter widths of between 1 15/16in (49mm) and 1 5/8in (41mm).

16. Sliding bevel. This tool is used for setting our angles, or bevels. Available in blade sizes of 9in (230mm), 10½in (270mm) and 12in (300mm).

17. Bradawl. This is a chisel pointed boring tool used for marking screw positions and counterboring for small size screws.

18. Adjustable steel rule. The pocket size variety, when fully extended, range in length from 6ft (1·83m) to 12ft (3·66m). The larger varieties are available in either steel, fiberglass or fabric in lengths of up to 100ft (30·5m).

19. Try square. This is used for setting out right angles and for testing edges when planing lumber square. The tool has a sprung steel blade and the stock is protected by a thin strip of brass or other soft metal. Available in blade lengths of 6in (150mm), 7½in (190mm), 9in (230mm) and 12in (300mm).

20. Marking gauge. This is used to mark one or more lines on a piece of lumber, parallel to one edge of that lumber. The type shown here is a mortise gauge which has a fixed point on one side and one fixed and one adjustable point on the other. Its specific use is for marking out mortise and tenon joints but it can be used in the same way as an ordinary marking gauge.

21. Folding wooden rule. This tool is also available in plastic. Primarily for joinery and carpentry use, it should be used narrow edge on to the lumber for the most accurate marking. These rules are available in 2ft (600mm) and 3ft (1m) sizes.

22. Scriber marking knife. One end of this tool is ground to a chisel shaped cutting edge for marking lumber. The other end is sharpened to a point and can be used for scribing metal.

23. Punch or nail set. This tool is used for tapping tack and nailheads below the surface of lumber. A range of head sizes is available to suit all nail sizes.

24. Center punch. This is used for spot marking metal to give a guide for drilling. The point is marked by tapping the wide end of the tool with a hammer. Automatic center punches (not shown) are available. These are spring loaded so you do not have to tap the end of the tool.

25. Carpenter's pencil. This has an oblong shaped lead which is sharpened to a chisel edge so that it can be used to black in lines scribed on lumber.

26. Posidrive type screwdriver. This tip is designed for use with Posidrive type screws which are increasingly replacing screws with the conventional blade head. The Posidrive screwhead allows far greater contact between the screwdriver tip and the screwhead — providing of course that the correct size of screwdriver tip is used. This makes for greater torque (twisting power) and reduces the likelihood of tool slip and consequent damage to the work.

27. Screwdriver. This tool is available in blade lengths of between 3in (75mm) and 18in (457mm) and tip widths of between 3/16in (4·8mm) and ½in (13mm). The screwdriver tip should fit the screw slot completely and the risk of tool slip will be further reduced if the screwdriver tip has been cross ground.

28. Carpenter's chisels. These are avilable

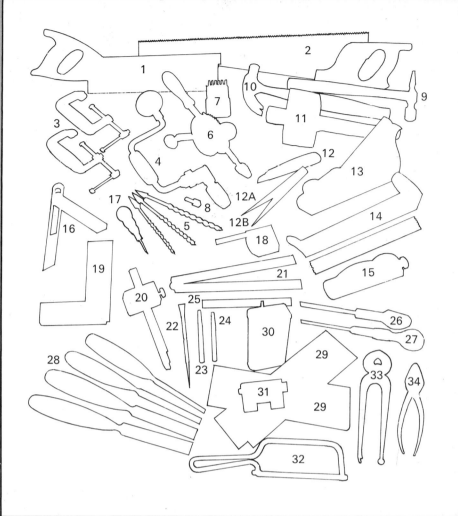

in several shapes and sizes of both handles and blades. The firmer bevel edge chisels shown here are probably the most useful all round chisels to have in a basic tool kit. Chisel handles are either of ash, boxwood or plastic (shown here). Plastic handles are virtually unbreakable on quality chisels but timber handles should be treated with care and should only be hit with a wooden mallet. Blade widths vary from 1/8in (3mm) to 2in (50mm).

29. Oilstones. These are used for sharpening the cutting edges of such tools as planes and chisels. There are two main kinds of oilstone, natural and artificial. Natural stone comes in several types. *Washita* gives a good finish and cuts well. *Arkansas* is an expensive stone but it is of high quality and produces a very fine edge. These are the most commonly used natural oilstones. Artificial stones come in three grades — coarse, medium and fine — and have the advantage of maintaining their quality. They are available in a selection of sizes including 5in x 2in (125mm x 50mm), 6in x 2in

(150mm x 50mm), 8in x 2in (200mm x 50mm), 10in x 2in (250mm x 50mm) and 8in x 1 7/8in (200mm x 45mm).

30. Fine machine oil. This has many lubricating uses in the workshop and is a reasonable substitute for Neatsfoot oil when using an oilstone.

31. Honing gauge. This is a useful device for holding bladed tools at the correct angle for sharpening on an oilstone. The disadvantage of this tool is that it tends to cause wear in the centre of the oilstone rather than distributing the wear evenly over the whole stone.

32. Small hacksaw. This is a general purpose saw for light metalworking jobs.

33. Pincers. These are used for pulling nails and tacks from lumber. If possible, always place a scrap of waste lumber between the jaws of the pincers and the work piece to avoid bruising.

34. Slip-joint pliers. This tool has a thin section so that the jaws can reach into tight places. It has two jaw opening positions and shear type wire cutter.

Begin with a box-on-wheels

Storage boxes can make very attractive items of furniture, in addition to being extremely practical. The modern tendency toward smaller houses and rooms means that storage planning becomes increasingly important. When articles are inconvenient to store in one place, the problem can often be overcome by using storage boxes. This basic unit affords scope for personal design and it is easy and inexpensive to make.

This unit, because of its simple structure, is a good introduction to carpentry. The work involved provides practice in the basic technique of glued and nailed butt joints, and the use of some important tools. Basically all furniture is of either frame or box construction. As the storage box uses both methods, the experience of making it will assist the handyman in a wide variety of projects later on.

If the box is required for several purposes its interior may have to be divided. Three different uses are illustrated here, and many more variations could be added. Handles can be attached, and the surfaces can be painted, polished, or covered with material or wallpaper.

Buying tools

When buying tools, quality is a prime consideration. With striking or impelling tools, such as a hammer or screwdriver, an inexpensive item will often serve – although there is nothing more annoying, when you are halfway through a job and the stores are closed, than having a hammerhead part permanently from its handle. But with saws, chisels and other cutting tools, the best buy is the best you *can* buy. In the long run, you will save money.

In this and subsequent chapters, the tools listed have been chosen to give the maximum versatility for the handyman who wants real 'mileage' for the money he spends on equipment.

Tools required

The tools needed for making the wheeled storage box are:

Carpenter's folding rule either 3ft or 1m long. Since building materials can be bought in metric sizes as well as standard sizes, a rule marked with both is handiest. For longer measurements, as when making fitted furniture, a *steel tape* is used. The best sort has a square case measuring exactly 2in across; it is handy for taking 'inside' measurements – for example, across the back of

an alcove.

Try square with a fixed blade. This is essential for seeing that lumber is square and for marking lines at right angles to the edges. Eight inches (203mm) or 9in (228mm) is the most useful size; it is wide enough to cover most shelves, for example, but not too unwieldly to use on a narrow molding.

Marking knife for scoring lines across the grain of the wood. It marks more accurately than a pencil and, by severing the fibers on the wood surface, helps ensure a clean cut with saw or chisel. A handyman's knife, such as the Stanley model with replaceable blades, will serve both as a marking knife and for several other jobs.

Panel saw about 22in (550mm) long with ten points (teeth) to the inch. It is designed for finishing work, such as cutting moldings, but will serve in a pinch for almost anything – from ripping (down the grain) or crosscutting (across the grain) in heavy lumber down to quite fine bench work.

Tenon saw about 12in (305mm) long with 14 points to the inch. The tenon saw has a stiffening rib along the back of the blade to help you cut a dead straight line. Used for fine cutting, it is essential if your ambitions lie in furniture making.

Bench hook to hold lumber steady when using a tenon saw. It is usually homemade (see instructions below).

Plane. There are many different types of

plane, but the handyman's most versatile tool, is a smoothing plane about 9¾in (250mm) long with a 2in (52mm) cutting edge. The Stanley No. 4 is a good example.

Claw hammer for driving and removing nails. Hammers come in several patterns and weights, and should be chosen to suit the individual's strength. An 8oz or 10oz will probably be best.

Bradawl for making 'start holes' for screws, in the absence of a drill.

Screwdriver about 10in (254mm) long, to fit No. 6 screws.

Nail punch to drive nailheads below the surface of the wood. When the punch holes are filled and smoothed down, a better surface is obtained than with exposed nailheads. Nail punches are also used for a variety of other jobs, for example:– to make 'start holes' for the electric drill in awkward situations; to loosen the heads of old screws that the screwdriver cannot budge; and in skew-nailing, to prevent the hammerhead from bruising the side of the lumber. Since punches are inexpensive, a range of three or four sizes is a useful investment.

The bench hook

Carpenters use the bench hook (Fig. 1 is an exploded diagram) to hold lumber steady while they are cutting it with a tenon saw. The length of batten or planking is held firmly against the upper 'lip' or edge, while the lower lip prevents the hook from slipping across the table or workbench. Since the upper lip is cut at an exact right angle, the experienced carpenter uses it as a guide while he cuts a straight line 'by eye'.

Although bench hooks can be purchased, they are so simple to make that it is usual to see the homemade variety in a workshop. And if you are starting off at carpentry, making a bench hook will show you how to measure, mark, cut and fasten lumber without a disaster – if you make a bad job, you can afford to throw it away and start again.

For materials, you need a rectangle or wood about 12in x 10in x 1in thick (or 300mm x 250mm x 25mm) and two pieces of batten 2in x 1in (or 50mm x 25mm) about 8in (or 200mm) long. But the dimensions are not critical: somewhere about this size will do.

Offcuts of wood are quite good enough, but make sure that none is warped; otherwise, the hook will rock and cause inaccurate cutting.

Measuring and marking

'Measure twice, cut once' is the first principle of carpentry. It saves a lot of waste!

When measuring with a folding rule (or any other measuring stick of considerable thickness), always stand the rule on edge so that the lines on the rule actually touch the lumber at the points where you want to mark it (Fig. 2). This will avoid sighting errors of the kind shown.

Lumber is almost never exactly straight. So you will find, if you try to mark right around a board

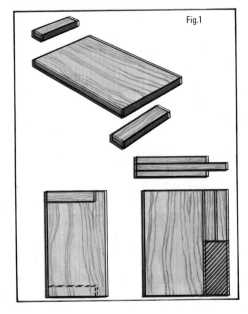

Fig.1

Right. *Burlap for the 'bar', paint for the toy box, felt for the sewing box – each box is finished to suit its intended use.*

Fig. 1 (left). *An exploded view of the bench hook. This can be cut from offcuts of any reasonably good lumber.*

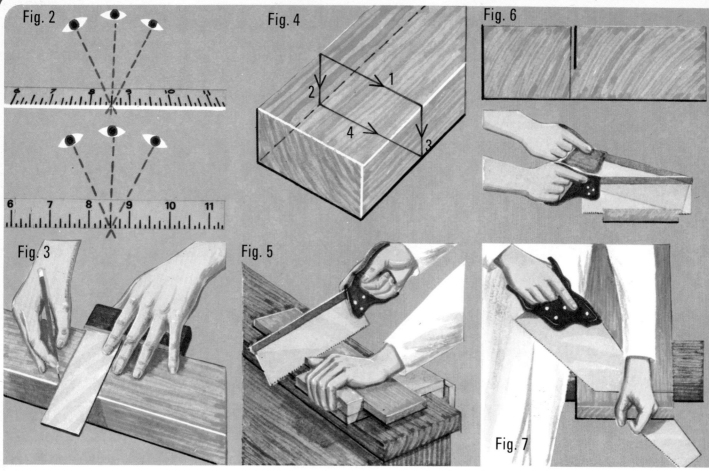

Fig 2. *If the rule markings are not touching the surface of the wood, inaccuracies will result. A folding rule, because of its thickness, is more likely to create this problem.*
Fig 3. *The correct method of using the try square and marking knife or pencil.*

Fig 4. *How to mark a sawing line around a piece of lumber. Note that lines 1 and 4, and 2 and 3, run in the **same** direction. This helps ensure a dead square cut.*
Fig 5. *Using the tenon saw and bench hook. Start by steadying the blade with your left thumb while you draw it back a few times.*

Fig. 6. *Start the saw cut with the blade at an angle of 45°. As you proceed, gradually lower it until it is almost horizontal.*
Fig. 7. *Using a panel or crosscut saw. Steady the work with your left hand until the offcut is nearly severed, then hold the offcut to prevent it splintering away.*

in a continuous line before cutting it, that you usually finish at a different point from where you started; the slight error caused by the curve in the board has 'compounded'. On a piece of planed 'inch by inch', the variation will probably be negligible. But on rough-sawn heavy lumber – a 2 x 4, say – you could easily find yourself $\frac{1}{8}$in or even $\frac{1}{4}$in out of line. The problem then becomes, 'Where *do* I cut?', and some poor joints can result.

So it is good practice to get into the habit of marking always in the correct order (Fig. 4).
The first stage of making the bench hook, then, is to mark a 'good' end on each of the battens. Use the try square as shown in Fig. 3, pushing it against the lumber with the thumb of your left hand and holding the blade flat with your fingers. Hold the blade of the marking knife against the blade of the try square, and score a line towards you across the lumber. Working in the order given above (you will have to swap hands at one stage), score lines on the other three surfaces.

Using the tenon saw

The next stage is to use the tenon saw to cut the batten. Since you have no bench hook – yet

– you will need a substitute (the chopping board, clamped to the table with the mincer?) and perhaps some help to hold the work steady. What you will try to do is to saw on the waste ('wrong') side of the marked line, so that the line is just barely visible after the cut is made. In fact, you should *always* cut on the waste side of the line, not down the middle; this avoids the possibility of cutting 'short'.

Hold the tenon saw with its teeth almost parallel with the surface of the wood (Fig. 5). Use your left thumb to guide the blade while you make your starting cut by drawing the saw backwards two or three times. Now try to saw smoothly and easily, using as much length of saw as possible for each stroke and letting the weight of the saw do the work (short, jerky strokes and heavy pressure will simply make the line crooked). Keep your line of vision over the saw to help you cut straight. When you reach the bottom of the cut, use three or four extra strokes to make sure you do not leave a fringe of fibers protruding.

If at your first attempt you have cut a squared line, the marking line will still be faintly visible all around. If not, call this the 'bad' end of the batten – and start again!

Once you have two battens with true ends, use the same marking and cutting process to square the ends of the 12in x 10in board. This time, use the panel saw, holding it at a slightly 'steeper' angle.

Nailing

If you 'can't drive a nail straight', do not worry – carpenters seldom do, either. A nail driven straight does not always have great holding power. So, in most jobs, alternate nails are driven at opposing angles for greater strength. For the bench hook, you should use the technique known as 'dovetail nailing'. There are several other techniques, but we shall begin with this one. Since the hook will have to withstand considerable pressure in use, you will need six 1¼in (31mm) nails, plus wood adhesive, for each batten.

Start by placing one batten along the top left-hand corner (as you look down at it) of the hook board, and drive one nail at each end until it is just catching the board below. Make sure you hold the nail firmly between thumb and forefinger, because the greater the length of nail that is held firmly the less likely it will be to bend. Drive with a short upswing and a full

Fig. 8

Fig. 9

Fig. 8. *When sawing heavy lumber, take a hold on the offcut when you are near the end of the sawing line.*
Fig. 9. *A suitable temporary support for sawing a large panel. There are many other ways in which you could improvise an adequate support.*

'follow-through', for the same reason. If the hammer tends to 'skid' off the nails it is probably because the face is dirty; clean it by rubbing it with a piece of sandpaper.

With your first two nails part-driven, lift the batten off the base and spread some adhesive thinly along it. Replace the batten, check that it is properly aligned – the partly driven nails will stop it skidding around on the glue – and drive home the two nails. On the last few hammer strokes in particular, try to keep the face of the hammer parallel with the wood surface, to lessen the risk of hammer 'bruises'. Now drive in the four intermediate nails.

The opposite batten is fastened on in the same way as the first. Note that it, too, goes on the left-hand side and not (unless you are ambidextrous!) diagonally opposite the first one.

Materials for the storage box

The storage box has dimensions of 2ft 2in x 1ft 6in x 1ft 4in (66mm x 457mm x 407mm). The complete body can conveniently be cut from a piece of 6ft by 3ft (or 2m x 1m) plywood, although a partitioned box would need a larger sheet. For a box this size plywood, ½in (13mm) thick is required. If cutting the panels is too

difficult, ask your local lumber dealer to cut them, using the dimensions in Fig. 10 as a guide.

In addition to the panels, you will need two 7ft 6in (2·4m) lengths of 2in by 1in (or 50mm by 25mm) wood batten; several dozen 1¼in (31mm) long nails; four castor wheels with screws; one tube of wood adhesive. Assemble all these materials first.

Cutting the panels

The panels are first marked out on the sheet plywood; then cut; then planed down slightly to the marked size.

If you intend cutting the panels from a single sheet, measure the outlines according to Fig. 10. Use the try square and marking knife for marking at right angles to the edges. Then extend the lines with the rule and marking knife. You must allow enough space between the panels for both the saw cut and for planing – ⅛in should be adequate. If you have no other straight-edge long enough to cover the longer dimensions, use the 'manufactured' edge of the first panel you cut out as a check that your other lines are straight.

The fine-toothed panel saw listed above is well suited for cutting plywood. A coarser saw, with fewer teeth or 'points' to the inch, would produce bad splintering along each side of the cut. Before beginning to cut, ensure that the plywood is placed on a suitably smooth surface that will not rock or slip, and that the line the saw blade has to travel is clear of obstructions. Accurate sawing requires a good working posi-

tion. Like the tenon saw, the panel saw demands an easy, flowing movement. Your job is to guide, withdraw and steady the saw; the cutting action comes from the saw's own weight.

As you near the end of the saw cut, you will need someone to hold the panel you are cutting off so that it does not wrench away from the sheet and leave great splinters. You cannot solve this problem by laying the sheet across two planks and sawing down the middle; the sheet will merely sag inwards into a slight V-shape and jam the saw.

Cut the two sides, two ends, and transverse partition (matching the ends) if wanted; but do not cut the top or bottom yet. Leave these until the box is assembled, when you can adjust their size to match any slight variation in your outer 'walls'.

Using 1¼in long nails and glue, nail the 2in x 1in castor fixing battens to the underside of the base (see side view on plan). Next, nail the ends to the base (again see side view on plan) and then nail the sides to the assembly.

Fig. 10. *The plywood sheet : an exploded view showing the cut panels in order of assembly. 'Label' each panel with a pencil before starting work. Note that the end panels must be shorter than the side panels by the thickness of the lid. Check this before cutting, otherwise the finished lid will not sit flush with the side panels, and you will have unnecessary planing to do.*

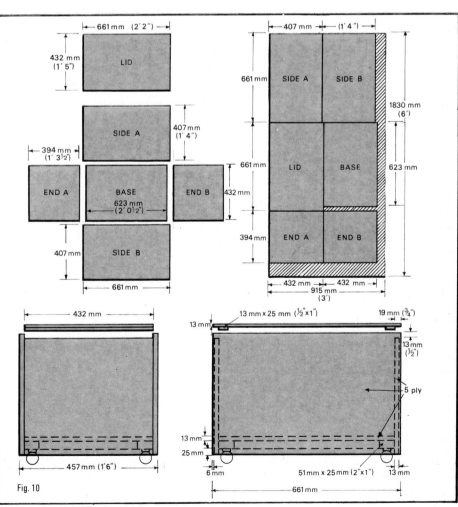

Fig. 10

A storage unit

This storage unit combines style and utility in a simple and compact design. It holds 11 drawers of four different sizes, yet maintains its overall neatness by the clever planning of the handles to give a uniform effect. The unit is designed to hold your possessions neatly and is invaluable in the workshop or studio. Once you have mastered this design you can add more units specifically planned to your requirements. In this way you can give your home lots of neat looking, inexpensive storage.

Assembly of the storage unit is straightforward, but as with all the designs in this series make sure you have all the required tools and materials. Check that your wood is of the right thickness and familiarize yourself with the various construction steps.

Preparations

Do not measure or cut the wood for the outer frame or body till you have made the drawers. This is because there will be small variations in the sizes of the drawers caused by unavoidable errors in cutting. The method by which you measure and cut out the body is detailed at a later stage.

Making the drawers

Carefully measure and mark out the wood to be used for the drawers and cut to the sizes given in the cutting list. The list shows the panel sizes of the different drawers and it will help if you keep the wood needed for each of the four sizes of drawer separate. When you are sure you have classified each panel correctly, sand them lightly with fine sandpaper.

Begin by making the three large drawers which all have the same dimensions. Take one of the back panels and glue and nail it between the two side panels, with the edge of the back panel flush with the ends of the side panels. This procedure applies with all the drawers — the

Above. Versatile and neat, this storage unit will prove invaluable to those with hobbies. Photographers, carpenters, needlwworkers and those who simply like hoarding things can store their possessions neatly in drawers of different shapes and sizes.

back panel is always held between the side panels.

Add the bottom by gluing and nailing. To ensure that the correct width between the sides is left for the front panel, hold this piece in position while you fix the bottom on. The front panel is not fixed until you have attached the handle to it. When you have made three sides of the drawer and the bottom, put it aside and assemble the other drawers in the same way.

Making the handles

Next, with a compass, mark out six 2¾in (70mm) diameter circles on 6mm plywood and cut these out with a jigsaw. Don't try and cut a perfect circle — few people can — but leave a narrow rim around the circle which can be sanded down to the mark with a fine grade of sandpaper. Then round off the front edge of the handles.

These handles are screwed to six smaller (40mm) circles which, because they will be hidden, need not be cut out so exactly. Glue the smaller circles to the backs of the handles making sure they are centered and use ⅜in long nails to secure them. Cut one circle into four equal quarters and another two into halves as handles for the smaller drawers.

To fix the handles to the front panels, screw them on from behind, making sure they overlap correctly so that the edges of the handles will be flush with the edges of the sides or tops of the drawers. This is best achieved by temporarily placing the front panels in position using a couple of drops of glue and gluing the handles on in the correct position. When the glue has set, take out the front panels and use $\frac{5}{8}$in No. 4 screws to fix the handles securely. For the small quarter handles use one screw only for each handle. Finally, fix the front panel in position and nail.

Measuring the body

The width of the top and bottom panels is $7\frac{7}{8}$in (200mm) which allows the drawers to be recessed. To find the exact length, measure the width of the three large boxes and add this measurement to the total width of the four 6mm uprights, plus 6mm. This last figure represents the space allowed between the three drawers and the uprights. Mark out the lines representing the uprights allowing 1mm on each side of the drawer. The same measurements are used for the top panel.

By the same method, mark out the measurements of the center shelf. This piece is 4mm shorter at each end — 8mm overall and this means that the positions of the vertical guides are calculated from 2mm inside each end of the shelf.

Measure the two sides by taking the height of top and bottom drawers together, and allowing 4mm for clearance and 6mm for the center shelf. Because the two inner uprights are housed in 2mm deep grooves cut in the top and bottom panels they are 4mm longer than the sides.

The length of the back panel is the same as the length of the top and bottom panels. Its height the same as the sides. There is a 4mm shelf inside the top left and right-hand spaces. Each of these shelves is $6\frac{3}{4}$in (170mm) deep and is equal in length to the distance between uprights plus 4mm for housing.

Assembling the body

The body is assembled on an 'egg-crate'

Below. *An exploded diagram of one end of the unit. The 'egg-crate' principle on which the body is assembled is shown, as are the grooves in the sides, in which the shelves are housed.*

principle. The uprights slot into the center shelf and are housed into the top and bottom panels. The center shelf is housed in the two side panels. Both the small upper shelves are housed in the sides and uprights. When you have marked out and cut the body to size, cut out the slots in the center shelf and inner uprights. Two slots $3\frac{7}{8}$in (98.6mm) long and just wide enough to take the uprights are cut in the center shelves where the two uprights meet it. A corresponding slot is cut in the uprights where the center shelf meets them.

With a sharp cutting tool such as a Stanley knife, cut square grooves 2mm deep in the appropriate places on sides, top, and bottom panels and uprights, to house the center shelf uprights, and small shelves respectively. First score the lines out to the correct width and depth and peel back the two layers of plywood. You are now ready for the final assembly. Glue and nail the two sides to the bottom panel. Assemble the center shelf and uprights by means of the slots and glue this piece into the housings on the side and bottom panels. Glue the two small shelves in place and glue and nail on the top panel and back panel, flush with the bottom and sides.

The assembly is now complete, the final stage is to lightly sand the unit and paint it in the colors of your choice. Paint the handles a different color from the main body and drawers to give a pleasing contrast.

CUTTING LIST

Solid wood	Standard (ft & in)	Metric (milli- meters)
For the drawers:		
1 strip 6mm plywood	$11'1\frac{7}{8}'' \times 2\frac{1}{8}''$	3400 x 53
1 strip 6mm plywood	$9'10\frac{1}{8}'' \times 4\frac{1}{2}''$	3000 x 116
1 strip 6mm plywood	$3'8\frac{1}{2}'' \times 7\frac{1}{8}''$	1130 x 180
This is cut and labelled as follows:		
(a) 8 panels	$2\frac{1}{4}'' \times 2\frac{1}{8}''$	57 x 53
(b) 12 panels	$7\frac{1}{16}'' \times 2\frac{1}{8}''$	180 x 53
(c) 4 panels	$5\frac{1}{8}'' \times 2\frac{1}{8}''$	129 x 53
(d) 4 panels	$2\frac{1}{4}'' \times 4\frac{9}{16}''$	57 x 116
(e) 10 panels	$7\frac{1}{16}'' \times 4\frac{9}{16}''$	180 x 116
(f) 6 panels	$5\frac{1}{8}'' \times 4\frac{9}{16}''$	129 x 116
(g) 6 panels	$2\frac{3}{4}'' \times 7\frac{1}{16}''$	70 x 180
(h) 5 panels	$5\frac{9}{16}'' \times 7\frac{1}{16}''$	142 x 180
1 large drawer: 2 x f	2 x e	1 x h
1 vertical half drawer: 2 x d	2 x e	1 x g
1 lateral half drawer: 2 x c	2 x b	1 x h
1 quarter drawer: 2 x a	2 x b	1 x g

Calculate the exact dimensions of the body after you have assembled the drawers, following the instructions given in the text.

The approximate dimensions are:

1 strip 6mm plywood	$4'11\frac{3}{4}'' \times 7\frac{7}{8}''$	1500 x 200

giving the sides, top, and bottom.

1 strip 6mm plywood	$18\frac{1}{2}'' \times 10\frac{1}{4}''$	470 x 260

giving the back.

1 strip 6mm plywood	$18\frac{1}{2}'' \times 7\frac{7}{8}''$	470 x 200

giving the center shelf.

1 strip 4mm plywood	$6\frac{1}{4}'' \times 6\frac{5}{8}''$	160 x 170

giving the small shelves.

You will also require:
Rip saw. Jig saw. Fine grade of sandpaper. Hammer. About 230 $\frac{5}{8}$in panel pins and small punch. 18 $\frac{5}{8}$in No. 4 screws. Cutting knife, such as a Stanley knife. Compass. Glue. Try square for measuring. Paint.

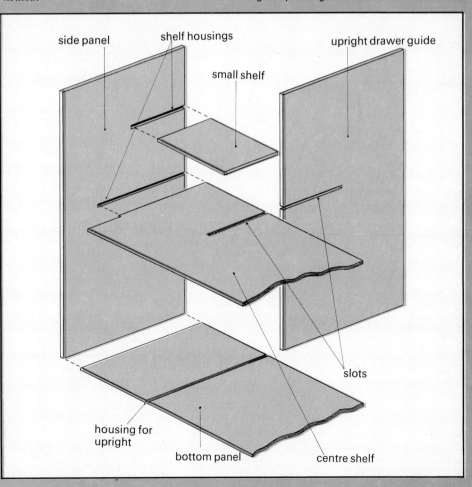

side panel / shelf housings / upright drawer guide / small shelf / slots / housing for upright / bottom panel / centre shelf

things to do in a day

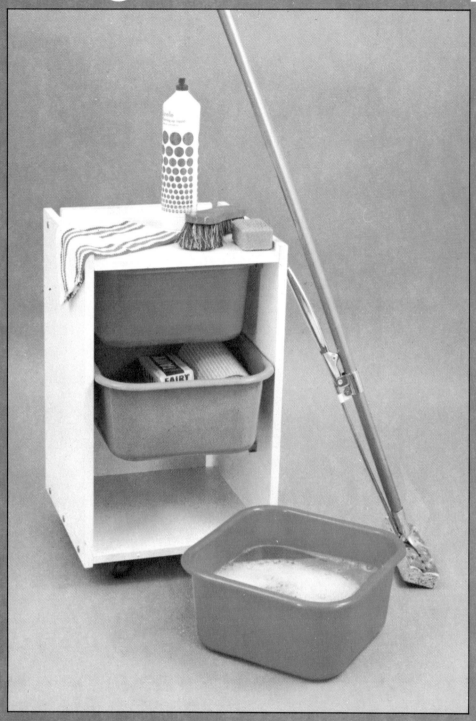

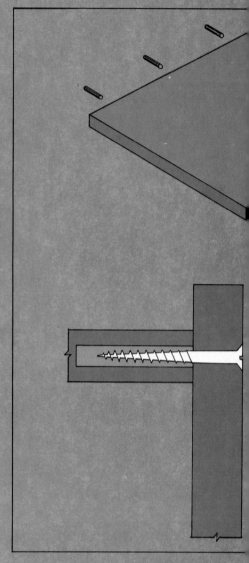

Storage unit on wheels

Storage units are among the most useful items of furniture. The trouble is, they are usually difficult or impossible to move, which greatly restricts their use. This particular unit has castors fitted, allowing you to move it to the location where it is most needed. And it can be built to dimensions that will suit the uses you have in mind.

This unit is constructed with chipboard covered with plastic laminate, but other materials can be used. For example blockboard, laminboard – both of which should be painted – and solid wood panels. One of the makes of wood-vaneered chipboard will also give an attractive finish.

All the panels can be cut from one sheet of 8ft x 15in material, but if you are at all unsure about being able to cut accurate right angles, ask your local lumber dealer or hardware store to do this for you.

Construction is very simple, especially the drawer arrangement, and the front has been left open to facilitate access; but if you prefer, a door could be fitted. The drawers are only dishpans, but you might like to use some of the prefabricated drawer kits on the market.

All the joints are simple butts. If a material with limited holding power for screws, such as chipboard, is used, it will be necessary to drill out all screw hole recesses to take equivalent sized fiber screw plugs. These plugs are tapped into place after a dab of woodworking adhesive has been squeezed into the hole. This provides a secure location for the screw heads.

Where screwheads are visible, covered-head or capped screws are used for a more attractive effect.

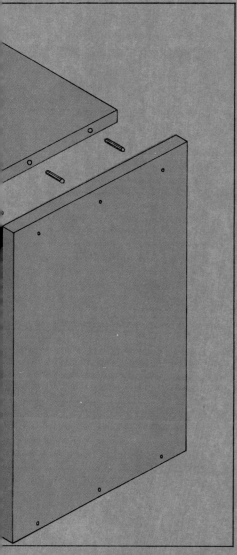

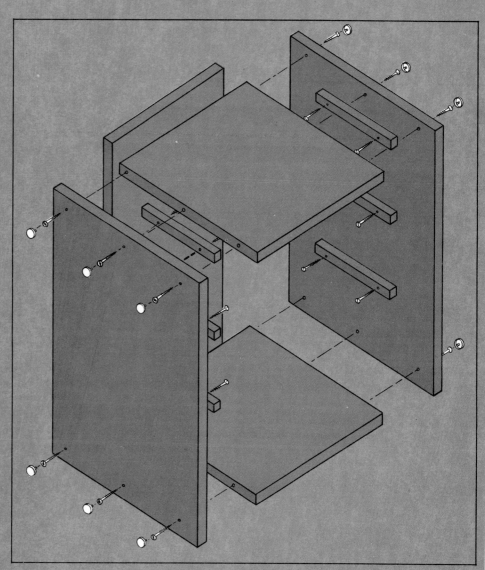

Above left. *If you make the unit from veneered chipboard, fiber plugs should be pushed into the screw holes to give an adequate fixing for the covered-head screws.*

Above right. *An exploded view of the storage unit. The dimensions of the components are given in the cutting list. Fit the unit with castors of your choice.*

Construction

Mark out the panels to the dimensions shown on the cutting list. This should be done with a fine-toothed panel saw to ensure a minimum of finishing and sanding down at the end. With a try square, check that all the panels are square at the corners, then do a 'dummy run' and assemble the parts to see that they fit properly.

Mark out the positions of the screw holes in all five panels, then drill these out. The holes in the edges of the top and bottom panels must be drilled to take fiber screw plugs.

If required, fit edging strip to all exposed edges.

Using a try square for accuracy, mark out the positions for the drawer runners. Then drill three screw holes along each runner, then line the runners along the marked lines and screw them firmly to the inside edges of the side panels.

Assemble the body – top, bottom and sides – first. This should be done on a flat surface,

using a try square to check each corner as you proceed. When this has been done, screw the back panel in position.

Next, fit the castors according to the manufacturer's instructions.

Castors often have to take considerable abuse, and there is considerable stress at this point. So if you are using chipboard it is best to screw them in place using glued fiber plugs, as described above, for fixing.

Finishing

The finish depends on the material used for construction. If laminated chipboard has been used, a wipe and polish is all that is required. But if something such as solid wood or blockboard has been used, you will have to sand down with a medium sandpaper, coat with a mixture of polyurethane and turpentine mixed 50/50, then sand down again with very fine sandpaper and finished with a coat of neat

polyurethane. This is perfect for solid wood with an attractive surface, but for plain wood, and sometimes blockboard, the material is not attractive enough for such treatment. In this case it is better to paint the unit.

You now have a portable storage unit, something that is both attractive and practical.

CUTTING LIST

Sections	Standard	Metric
2 side panels	$22\frac{1}{4} \times 15$	565 × 381
1 top panel	$13\frac{1}{4} \times 14\frac{3}{8}$	337 × 365
1 back panel	$22\frac{1}{4} \times 12$	565 × 305
6 runners	$7\frac{1}{2} \times \frac{5}{8} \times \frac{5}{8}$	190 × 16 × 16

You will also require: 3 rigid square plastic bowls or trays; 12 covered-head screws ($1\frac{1}{2}$ x No. 8); 6 $1\frac{1}{4}$ x No. 8 screws for fixing back; 12 fiber screw plugs; 1 set of castors of your choice; 12 1 x No. 8 round-head screws for fixing runners; woodwork adhesive. (Plastic edging strip if a laminate surface is used.) All standard measurements in inches, and all metric measurements in millimeters.

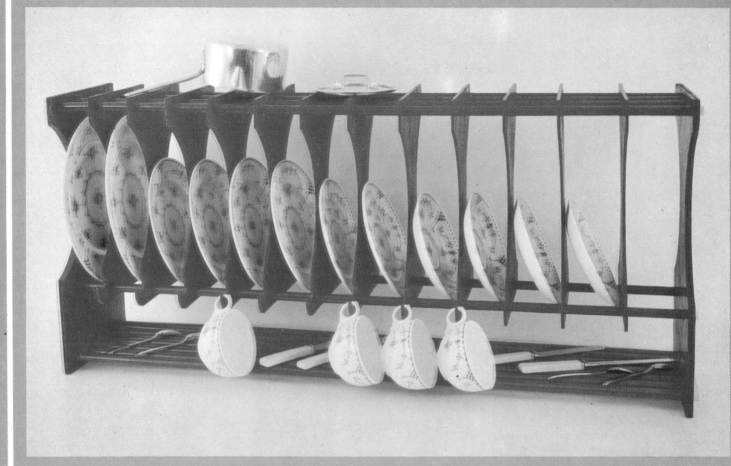

Versatile dish rack

This versatile rack can be used for the casual storage of dishes, records or magazines. You can probably think of several other items for which it could be used. It is easily constructed in a day, using wood dowelling and panels of plywood (or you could use hardboard).

Construction

The unit consists of two end panels of ⅝in plywood, and a series of inside panels of ⅜in plywood, joined by 13½in dowelling rods. Six of the rods pass through all the panels, and the remaining seven through the bottom of the end panels only. Complete construction details are shown in Fig. 1.

Nails or screws are not used in the construction. The rods are inserted through holes in the panels that are just large enough to pass through, and are held in place with a waterproof woodworking adhesive.

This unit has been designed as a dish rack,

The length of the unit is a matter of choice, and depends on the lengths of the dowelling rods and the number of compartments formed by the inside panels.

and for this reason a recess has been cut out of the lower front edge of each inside panel. These recesses allow cups and mugs to be hung along the front of the unit. This of course is not necessary if you want to use the unit for records or magazines.

The end and inside panels are marked using the outlines shown in Fig. 1. The ends are extended according to the dimensions listed. When all the panels are ready, they are placed together and holes drilled through all panels at the same time. This ensures that all the dowel holes are in perfect alignment.

Because the unit has many glued joints, the component parts should not be painted before assembly. On the other hand, the completed unit is very awkward to paint with a brush. This problem can be overcome by spraying with one of the aerosol-type paints.

Preparation

Transfer the outline shown in Fig. 1 onto tracing paper. This is the template for the curved outline of both end and inside panels.

Use this template to mark out the end panels. Place the template in position according to the dimensions shown in Fig. 1, so that there is a short 1½in flat section immediately above the top ends of the curves, as shown in Fig. 1.

Mark out, and cut, one end panel. Use this panel as a template for the opposite end panel and all the inside panels.

Mark out, and cut, the opposite end panel and the required number of inside panels.

When this has been done, sandwich all the panels together, with the two end ones on the outside, by aligning the curved and top edges.

Clamp the sandwich firmly together with two clamps. Fit a ½in bit in a drill and mark and drill the holes for the rods. The sandwich method enables you to drill a hole through several panels at once, ensuring exact alignment.

Assembly

'Thread' the rods through the panels and trial assemble the unit. Cut the dowelling to the final lengths. Move all the panels about ½in along the dowelling, spread adhesive around the rods near the panels, then move the panels back to their correct positions, over the adhesive. Leave for adhesive to set.

When the glue has set, sand down and paint or spray.

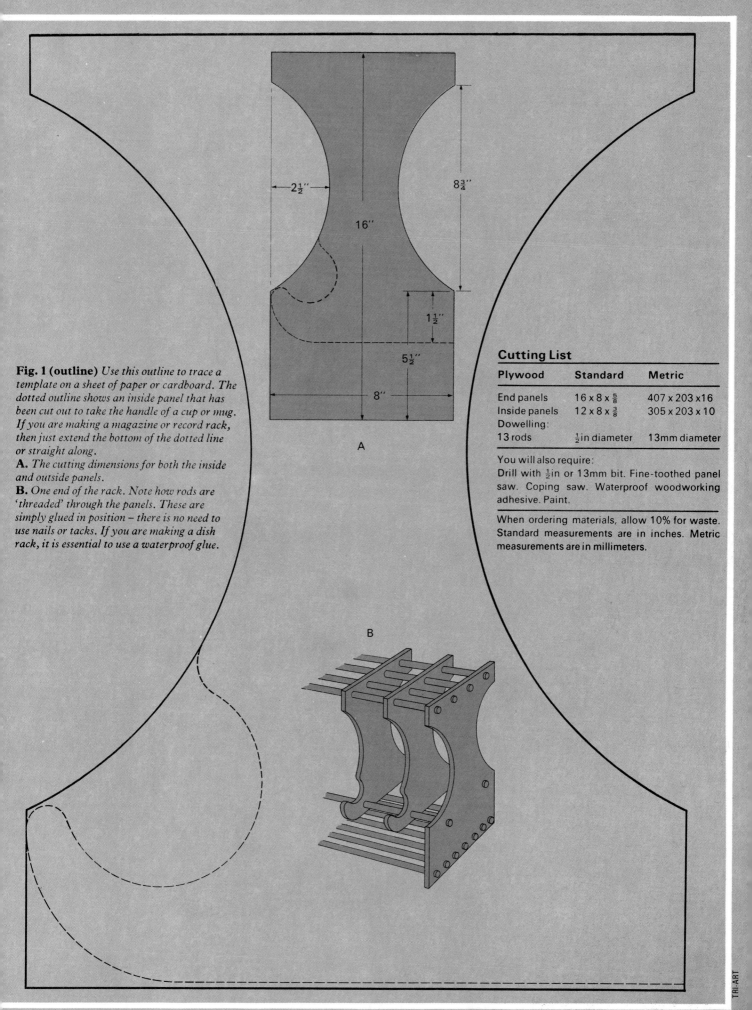

Fig. 1 (outline) *Use this outline to trace a template on a sheet of paper or cardboard. The dotted outline shows an inside panel that has been cut out to take the handle of a cup or mug. If you are making a magazine or record rack, then just extend the bottom of the dotted line or straight along.*
A. *The cutting dimensions for both the inside and outside panels.*
B. *One end of the rack. Note how rods are 'threaded' through the panels. These are simply glued in position – there is no need to use nails or tacks. If you are making a dish rack, it is essential to use a waterproof glue.*

A

B

Cutting List

Plywood	Standard	Metric
End panels	16 x 8 x $\frac{5}{8}$	407 x 203 x16
Inside panels	12 x 8 x $\frac{3}{8}$	305 x 203 x 10
Dowelling:		
13 rods	$\frac{1}{2}$in diameter	13mm diameter

You will also require:
Drill with $\frac{1}{2}$in or 13mm bit. Fine-toothed panel saw. Coping saw. Waterproof woodworking adhesive. Paint.

When ordering materials, allow 10% for waste. Standard measurements are in inches. Metric measurements are in millimeters.

TRI-ART

NIGEL MESSETT

Left. *Stocked with good looking spice jars, this simply designed and attractively finished spice rack will add a touch of country charm to your kitchen. The disks of the rack in the photograph are 8" in diameter. The height of the rack depends on the height of the spice jars you have.*

and circumference of the spice jars shown in the photograph. You can alter the dimensions to suit the type of spice jars you already have, or intend to buy.

Cutting the plywood disks

To make the plywood disks, first cut three pieces of plywood about 8½in x 8½in (216mm x 216mm). Draw in the diagonals in pencil on one of these pieces to locate its center. Take a compass and, from this center point, draw a circle with an 8in (203mm) diameter.

Put the three squares of plywood together with their surfaces butting and the marked-out piece on top, facing you. Put the pieces in a woodworking vise, with about half the area of the lumber standing proud.

Now cut out all three disks at once with a coping saw, moving the pieces around in the vise as necessary. Cut around the waste side of the pencilled circle. Then, with the disks still held together, shape the circumference with a spokeshave followed by sandpaper to give a smooth circumference.

If you have a powered jigsaw, this will do a better job in a fraction of the time.

The top disk

To make the top disk of the spice rack, take the plywood disk that you marked the center on earlier. The top disk has six cutouts spaced at equal intervals around its circumference.

The size of these cutouts depends on the diameter of the neck of the spice jars. You can measure this with a pair of dividers or, if you have them, outside calipers.

The procedure for marking out the top disk is straightforward. The center lines of the cutouts – (those that would run through the center of the disk) – are marked with a 30°–60° set-square which is laid on the disk with its bottom edge on the diagonal lines – now the center lines of the disk – that you have already marked. From the points where the center lines of the cutouts meet the edge of the disk, measure inward the required distance – this will partly be determined by the diameter of the spice jar necks. Make pencil marks at these points. Using these points as centers, draw circles that equal the diameter of the jar necks. Draw a line through the center of each circle, at right angles to the lines already marked with the set-square. From the point where these new lines intersect the circumference of the circles, draw straight lines to the edge of the disk.

Now drill small holes through the center of the marked circles. These holes are not used to make the cutouts – they are simply to help you mark the center of the rebates that are later in the middle base. Lay the top disk on the middle disk

Handy spice rack

If you have ever spent a frustrating time searching your kitchen shelves and cupboards for the spice that will add the perfect touch to a meal, this spice rack is for you. It will keep your favorite spices in one place so that you can find them immediately. The spice rack looks good, and can also be made in a day.

The spice rack consists of three 8in (203mm) diameter birch plywood disks. A ⁹/₁₀in (23mm) diameter dowel is fixed to the bottom disk through its center and runs through, but is not attached to, holes cut in the centers of the middle and top disks. A small plastic washer, which could be cut out of a vinyl tile, is slipped over the dowel and rests between the bottom and middle disks. This allows the middle and top disks to revolve so you can reach all the jars

easily.

U-shaped cutouts around the circumference of the top disk carry the necks of the spice jars. The bases rest in the circular rebates cut in the upper surface of the middle disk. The center pivot dowel is shaped at the top to provide a finger grip for lifting the spice rack.

Dimensions

The dimensions given here are for the height

and push a sharp pointed tool through the drill holes to mark the middle disk. A metalworking scriber or a bradawl will do for this job.

Put this middle disk to one side and make the cutouts in the top disk with a coping saw. Shape them to a smooth finish with a small, round file and sandpaper.

The middle disk

The middle disk has six $\frac{1}{8}$in (3mm) deep circular rebates cut in the top surface to accommodate the bases of the spice jars. The centers of these rebates match the centers of the cutouts in the top disk and have already been marked.

The best way of cutting the rebates is with a power router, but few handymen have these. You could use a Forstener bit, fitted to a brace to do the job, but these are expensive.

A good alternative method of construction that overcomes these problems is to make the middle disk from two sheets of plywood. The top sheet should be made of the thinnest plywood available – 2mm or 3mm. You can then drill right through this sheet and glue it to the other panel to give you one disk with rebates approximately $\frac{1}{8}$in deep.

To make the middle disk by this method, mark the circumference of the rebates on the thin sheet of plywood. Clamp this sheet in a vise with a piece of waste lumber backing it. Then either drill holes just inside the circumference of the circles and cut them out with a coping saw – you will have to cut through the waste wood as well – or cut through the thin plywood sheet only with a pattern bit fitted to a brace. If you choose this latter method you must cut out the hole from both sides of the plywood otherwise the sheet will twist and break. When you have made the holes, glue the thin sheet of plywood to the thicker sheet with a woodworking adhesive.

When the middle disk is complete, put it in a vise together with the top disk. Drill holes through both pieces for the three dowel rods that connect these disks. The position of the holes is shown in Fig. 1.

The center pivot

The center pivot is a length of $^9/_{10}$in (23mm) diameter dowel. At the bottom it is glued into a hole cut in the center of the base disk. The other two disks revolve around this pivot. A finger grip is cut in the pivot towards the top.

Cut the dowel to length and form the finger grip. You can turn this on a lathe or shape it with a chisel. Clamp all three disks together and, with a brace and bit, drill a $^9/_{10}$in hole through the center of all the pieces. Try to ensure that the sides of the hole are vertical, particularly for the one running through the bottom disk.

Glue the center pivot into the hole in the bottom disk with a woodworking adhesive. Make sure the pivot is vertical. With a small chisel, carefully ease the sides of the center holes in the middle and top disks so that they can revolve smoothly around the center pivot.

Now cut the three dowels that connect the

middle and top disk. These are $\frac{3}{8}$in (9·5mm) diameter and their length depends on the height of the spice jars. Glue these dowels in place in the holes already cut in the two disks.

Finishing

When the adhesive has dried, sandpaper all parts of the spice rack and apply a coat of clear varnish. Rub this down with steel wool for a smooth finish, then apply a final coat.

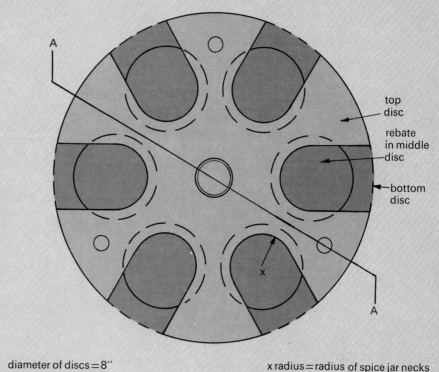

diameter of discs = 8''

x radius = radius of spice jar necks

Fig. 1

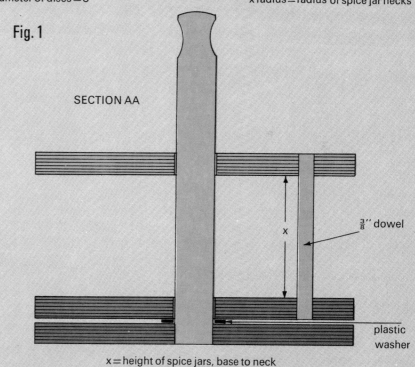

SECTION AA

$\frac{3}{8}$'' dowel

plastic washer

x = height of spice jars, base to neck

top disc

rebate in middle disc

bottom disc

Fig. 1. *A plan and section view of the rack.*

Now slip a plastic washer over the center pivot so that it rests on the bottom disk. Slide the middle and top disks onto the pivot so that they rest on the plastic washer. The top two disks should revolve freely.

All you need do now is fill the spice jars and label them. Your good-looking spice rack is now ready for use.

NIGEL MESSETT

Fold-down table

Space-saving furniture has become increasingly popular, especially in modern houses with a small 'box room' type bedroom or small kitchen area. This fold-down table is a simple idea that will expand your living space in any restricted area. The table is so easy to make that you can do the job in a day — and with a little more time, equip every room in the home.

Above. This simple space saver can be used as an occasional breakfast or dining bar or as a writing desk. The curved ends provide room for papers if you are writing at the table.

The shape of the table top is a matter of choice. The flap shown in the photograph has a curved area at both ends — ideal for holding papers if you are writing or typing at the table. The depth of the table from the front edge to the wall edge is important. If it is too shallow you will not be able to use the table as a desk. If you increase the depth of the table you will have to use larger folding brackets than the ones used here to support the top. Manufacturers of these brackets state the area they are capable of supporting — do not exceed this specification.

General construction

Only three pieces of lumber are needed for the table. The table top can be made of plywood, chipboard or blockboard. Plywood can be finished with clear varnish, blockboard and chipboard with plastic laminate or with decorative self-adhesive plastic sheeting. If you use plastic laminate, both the top and bottom surfaces must be covered — this 'balances' the panel and helps to prevent it warping.

Metal folding brackets are screwed to the underside of the table top and to wall support strips. These run at right angles to the table top. The support strips are made from 1in (25mm) softwood. The table is screwed to the wall, which must be plugged, through these support strips.

The brackets

There are several types of folding brackets on the market and hardware stores will have a selection. The brackets used for the table in the photograph lock when the table is lifted out. The lock 'breaks' to allow the top to be folded down when the table top is lifted upward slightly from the level horizontal position.

The table top

The table top can be made out of plywood, chipboard or blockboard — the marking out and cutting procedure is the same whatever material you use.

The first step is to cut a panel of the material you are using to the dimensions shown in Fig. 1. Mark the back edge — the edge that will butt the wall — and plane it square.

Now mark the curves on the ends of the panel. To do this, measure and mark a distance of 10in (250mm) — the radius of the curves — in from the ends of the panel. Square a line through these points. Then, along these lines from the front

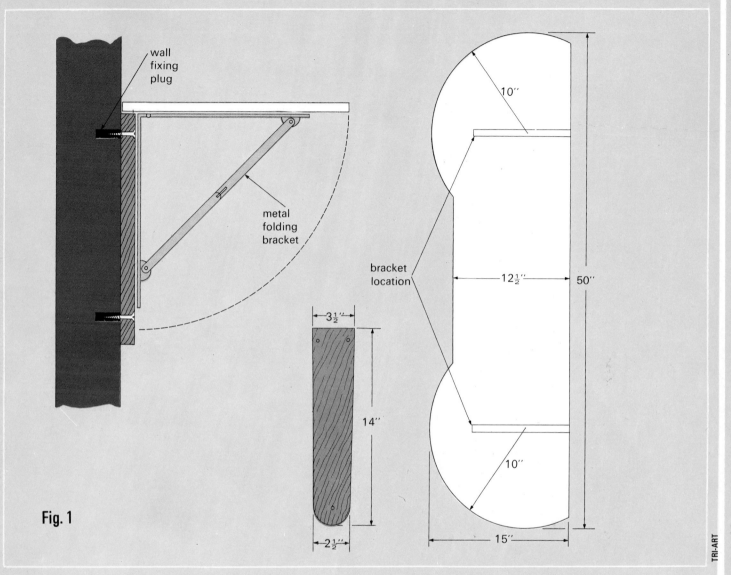

Fig. 1

TRI-ART

edge of the panel, measure and mark a distance of 10in (250mm). This point is the center of the circumference of the curves.

To mark the curves, tie a pencil or indelible marker to a length of string. Attach the other end of the string to a straight pin. Push the straight pin into the center mark. Swing the pencil round, marking the curve on the panel. Do this at both ends of the board.

The next step is to mark the central straight area in the front edge of the table top. This is $2\frac{1}{2}$in (63·5mm) in from the front of the end curves. You can mark this with a marking gauge or with a rule, straightedge and pencil.

Cutting the table top

The next step is to cut out the shape marked on the panel. You can do this with a power jig saw or with a coping saw. Cutting chipboard is a laborious job but a power jig saw, fitted with a coarse-toothed blade, will speed up the job. Finish the curves as neatly as you can with a spokeshave.

The table top can now be finished. If you are using plywood, simply smooth the surface with fine sandpaper and apply a coat of clear varnish. Rub this down with steel wool when dry and apply a second coat of varnish. If you are using plastic laminate on the table top, use the cutout panel as a template to mark out the two sheets of laminate. Cut these sheets out together with a coping saw, with a scrap piece of hardboard clamped behind them. Apply the laminate to the top panel with a contact adhesive and, when dry, cut down the edges with a spokeshave. Then apply edging strip to all edges.

The wall support strips

These are made from 1in (25mm) thick softwood. The supports taper slightly towards the bottom end, as shown in Fig. 1. Mark out and cut the support strips.

Assembly

Drill three holes in each of the wall support strips for 2in No. 8 countersunk screws. The position of these holes is shown in Fig. 1. Drill the wall where the table is to be fixed for fiber wall plugs. Position these so that the table, when fixed in place, will be about 28in (710mm)

from the floor – this is a comfortable height for a desk or dining bar. Screw the support strips to the wall.

Now screw the wall brackets to the support strips with $\frac{3}{4}$in No. 8 countersunk screws. Extend the brackets to the table-up position and lay the top panel on them. Make sure there is adequate clearance between the back edge of the panel and the wall. Mark on the underside of the panel the position of the holes which have to be drilled for fixing the top to the brackets.

Drill into the top panel for $\frac{1}{2}$in No. 8 countersunk screws. Make sure that you do not drill right through the panel – a drill stop or a piece of colored adhesive tape attached to the drill bit will prevent this. Screw the panel in place.

The fold-down table is now complete and ready for use. You will soon appreciate its advantages and, if you have a bit of time to spare, may wish to install one in other rooms.

Versatile coffee table

Above. *This coffee table has a top that can be lifted off and turned over to display a different color or pattern.*

The colors and patterns on furniture often have an inhibiting effect on the decor of the surrounding room. It is pointless, for example, having a living room decorated along Victorian lines if the surface of the coffee table is ablaze with psychedelic colours. The reversible top of this coffee table helps overcome this problem.

The top fits neatly into the frame and can be lifted off and turned over. If you cover one surface in a formal or traditional pattern, and the opposite side in a bright gay pattern or color, then you can adjust the top according to your mood or the surrounding decor. This is particularly useful if you wish to move the table into another room for a while. You could even make two table tops, giving you a choice of four different surfaces!

Construction

The construction outline is shown on Fig. 2. The main point to bear in mind is that the four side rails must be the same length as the long dimensions of the table top; in this case $17\frac{3}{4}$in or 451mm.

The base frame, as shown in Fig. 2, is very easy to make, and consists of four leg members joined by four rails. Two of the rails are fixed so that their top edges are below the tops of the legs at a depth equal to the thickness of the table top. The remaining rails are fixed at right angles to these, immediately underneath.

Two rails — the lower ones — are screwed through the long grain of the rails and into the long grain of the leg members. The top rails are secured by screwing through the long grain of the legs, into the end grain of the rails. Screwing or nailing into end grain does not provide a very strong joint, and for this reason the end grain of the top rails is drilled to take No. 8 size fiber screw plugs. These plugs are glued into the drilled holes and, when the adhesive has set, provide a strong fixing location for the screws. The procedure is shown in Fig. 1.

This top is of chipboard covered with a laminated plastic on both faces and on the edges. But you could use blockboard, plywood, or even solid wood if you prefer; with any suitable covering.

Assembling the frame

First cut the four legs. The length of each leg will be the eventual height of the surface of the table. So if you require a lower, or taller table, do this by cutting the legs to the desired length.

Next cut the rails. Use fine sandpaper to smooth down all surfaces, particularly the end grain, because this will be showing on some parts of the construction.

Now prepare the top. You may have purchased a laminated or veneered top already. If it is veneered with a particular wood on the two faces and the edges, you may wish to apply different veneer to one of the surfaces. In any case the top should have its final finish before you start to screw the frame together. In this way you can make any small alterations on the rail members at this stage.

Mark out and drill the holes for the screws. The two upper rails have to be drilled through the end grain. Squeeze a little glue into these holes, then press a fiber plug into each one.

Now make a trial assembly of the frame, driving the screws in lightly, and check that the table top drops snugly into the recess created by the tops of the legs and the two upper rails. Cut and adjust if necessary. When the fit is perfect, loosen the screws, add a little woodworking adhesive to the butting surfaces of each joint, then drive the screws firmly home.

Finishing

Sandpaper all surfaces to a smooth finish, then, with a soft cloth damped with mineral spirits, wipe all surfaces to pick up all the fine dust caused by sanding.

With a good quality 2in or 50mm brush, sparingly apply a varnish of clear matte polyurethane and turpentine, diluted 50/50. When dry, cut down with fine sandpaper. Wipe the surface with damp cloth again, re-coat with the same varnish mixture, and, when dry, finish by rubbing down with grade 4/0 or 0000 steel wool. Clean the surface with ordinary turpentine, or mineral spirits, leave an hour, then apply a coat of undiluted polyurethane.

When you have finished, you will have a coffee table that is both original and versatile.

Cutting list

Solid wood	Standard	Metric
4 legs	13 x 1¾ x ⅞	330 x 44 x 22
4 rails	17¾ x 1¾ x ⅞	451 x 44 x 22
Chipboard or plywood		
Table top	17¾ x 17¾ x 1	451 x 451 x 25

You will also require covering material (stick-on plastic sheet, plastic laminate or other veneers), or any other covering you may prefer.
16 1½in No. 8 screws with plastic screw caps. Fine sandpaper. Woodworking adhesive. Varnish or paint for the legs and rails. And 8 No. 8 fiber screw plugs.

All measurements are approximate — allow 10% for waste when ordering. Standard measurements in inches. Metric measurements in millimeters.

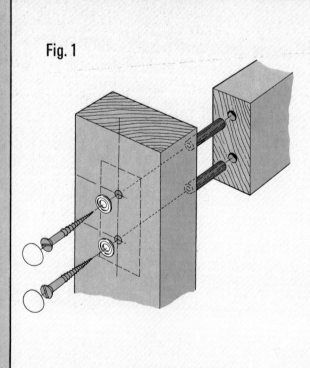

Fig. 1

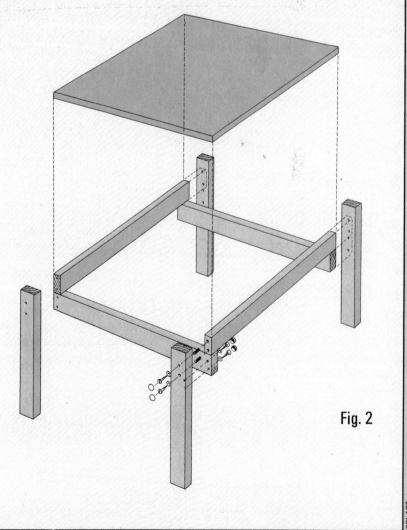

Fig. 2

Fig. 1. *To improve the holding power of end grain, holes are drilled that are large enough to take fiber screw plugs. These are glued in position to provide a strong fixing location for the screws.*
Fig. 2. *The unit consists of four vertical members, the legs, and four cross members acting as braces, two of which provide support for the reversible top. There are no complex joints in the construction, all joints are of the simple butting variety and are glued and screwed in place.*

things to do in a day

NIGEL MESSETT

A convertible stool

In modern homes, where rooms are small and space is at a premium, multipurpose units have a special attraction. This compact stool can be tucked under a breakfast or cocktail bar, or it can double as a telephone table, occasional table or writing desk. With minor modifications to the basic design you can turn the stool into an attractive and original coffee table.

Left. *Built to a modern design and brightly finished, this compact stool is ideal for use at a breakfast bar or dining table. Other useful items can be made by modifying the basic design – examples are shown opposite.*

Constructed entirely of $\frac{5}{8}$in (or 16mm) plywood, not only is the finished product strong, durable and attractive, but all surfaces are smooth-finished, giving it a professional look. It can be stained, veneered, painted, or covered with adhesive soft plastic sheet or hard plastic laminate.

Marking and cutting
The first step is to cut the two shaped side-panels to be used as the vertical supports (A and B), according to the dimensions given in Fig. 1.
Cut out the parts with a jigsaw or a hand keyhole type saw. When cutting curved lines do not work exactly to the mark, but leave a small margin which can be planed then sanded. In this final stage, place the two components together in a vise and shape the curved edges with a spokeshave or plane, then sand down with fine sandpaper.
From the remaining piece (see Fig. 1) mark out and cut a piece 15$\frac{1}{2}$in (394mm) wide. From this, mark off and cut the following pieces:
(C) Seat Top
(D) Seat Front Support
(E) Seat Rear Support
(F) Footrest
(G) Base, Front
Cut the sides a fraction overwide and plane to accurate dimensions. Clamp a piece of waste wood to the end to which you are planing – this prevents damage to the corners.

Construction
Onto each of the main panels, affix with screws and woodworking adhesive the specified lengths of $\frac{3}{4}$in (19mm) scotia or triangular wood molding in the positions shown in Fig. 1. In order to ensure a flush finish, make sure that the edge of the molding is fixed exactly at the width of the material ($\frac{5}{8}$in or 16mm) from the outer edge of the pieces.
The unit is now ready for assembly. Rest pieces A and B on their longest straight sides and fix pieces G and E into position, with screws and woodworking adhesive. Fix seat top (C); turn over and fix pieces F and D.
Using fine sandpaper, carefully smooth the completed unit, then add the finish desired. If you decide to paint it, first apply an undercoat then two coats of high-gloss polyurethane.

Upholstery
Make a cushion – rectangular or oval shaped – of colored material of your choice. A filling of 2in (50mm) thick foam rubber or polyester gives a trim finish and provides far greater comfort. A 'medium hard' consistency of foam is the best choice.

24

The completed unit in its basic form is now ready for use, and once you have seen this attractive example of the type of result you can obtain in plywood, you will be prompted to make other units in this versatile and inexpensive material.

With minor modifications, this unit can be transformed into a number of other handy items for the modern home. Here are some of the suggested uses:

Telephone table

On pieces A and B fix an 8in length of $\frac{3}{4}$in (19mm) scotia or triangular molding with screws and woodworking adhesive. Cut a piece of plywood 15$\frac{1}{2}$in x 8in (394 x 203mm), and fix into place as a shelf to hold the telephone directories.

Coffee table

Rest the unit on its 'front', thus using the seat and base as the table's 'legs'. Cut a sheet of $\frac{1}{2}$in (13mm) thick laminated or veneered hardboard measuring the overall dimensions of the unit. Fix with adhesive, suction cups, or screws from underneath.

If you wish to add a magazine rack, build a holder from strips of wood molding beneath the 'base end'.

Fig. 1. *An exploded view of the plywood stool with all the necessary dimensions.*
Fig. 2. *This one-day project gives you a multi-purpose unit—ideal in modern houses where space is limited. The diagram gives three ideas. The first, on the left, involves turning over the construction so that it rests on pieces E and F (Fig. 1.) A table top can then be fitted. The construction can also be used as a writing desk as shown in the centre. The shelf for telephone directories can be made from a sheet of plywood supported by lumber battens or lengths of triangular molding. These are fixed to the inside surfaces of pieces A and B (Fig. 1).*

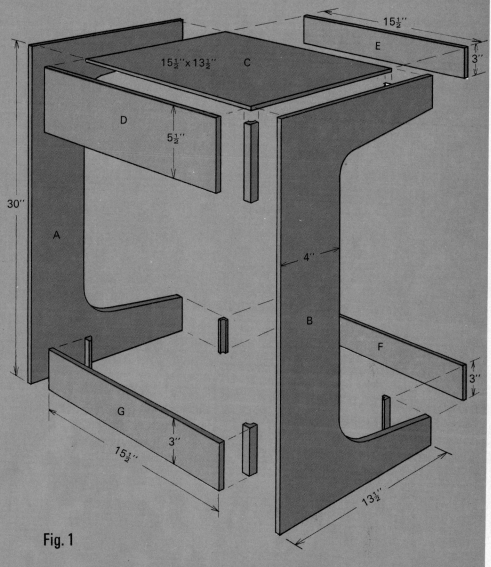

Fig. 1

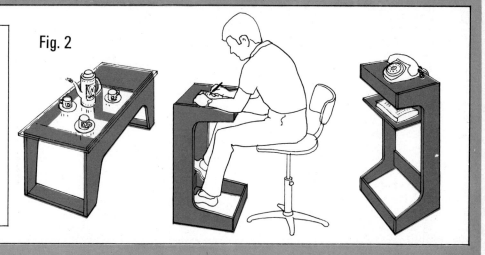

Fig. 2

Cutting list

Plywood	Standard	Metric
A $\frac{5}{8}$in or 16mm Panel	50 x 50 or smaller	1270 x 1270 or smaller

Cut to give: 2 vertical side-panels, 1 seat-top and four pieces as shown in the diagram.
You will also need 6ft (or 2m) $\frac{3}{4}$in (19mm) scotia or triangular wood molding.
Woodworking adhesive. Medium and fine sandpaper. Jigsaw or keyhole type saw. Paint or self-adhesive plastic laminate.

things to do in a day

Hardboard coffee table

An occasional table which folds away when not in use is ideal for small apartments. This attractive design is constructed entirely from laminated hardboard, a material which is both easy to work and long lasting. One of the other attractions of this piece is that no nails or screws are used in the construction so it is easily completed in a short time.

Hardboard is a much more versatile and adaptable material than is commonly realized. By laminating two panels of hardboard, back to back, a rigid and balanced sheet is produced which is ideal for a wide variety of constructions. This laminated hardboard is used for this occasional table and not only is the finished structure strong, but all surfaces are smooth and plain which allows an attractive finish.

One of the other features of the table is that it is portable and easily and quickly stored. This stems from the extremely simple method of construction which allows the legs to be removed in seconds. No screws or nails are used in the structure; the legs slot into each other and are held in the assembled position by two small flat door bolts which are glued to the underside of the table top.

Preliminaries

First decide what shape you want the table to be. The table illustrated and described in this article is made in a popular modern style but can be modified to individual preferences. Other atttractive designs include round, square or oval table tops, but whatever style you choose you will find that the laminated hardboard is easy to work.

The other consideration is 'finish'. You can paint the completed unit or cover it with a rigid plastic laminate. If you choose the laminate it is essential that you have enough to cover both sides of the table top in order to balance the material.

Conditioning the hardboard

If two laminated panels are to be used for constructing the table, they must be 'conditioned' by damping the backs of the panels and leaving them stacked, back to back, for 24 to 48 hours. Because of the delay between preparing the panels and actually constructing the table, decide on which day you want to build the table and buy and prepare the panels at least three days in advance. The only way in which the table can be prepared and constructed in one day is to use a single sheet of $\frac{1}{4}$in (6mm) thick hardboard. This material is just as strong as the laminated boards but one surface will be too rough to take a good finish. Whatever hardboard you use choose a hard-wearing grade. You can get advice from your lumber dealer.

Gluing and marking out

When the two panels have dried they are bonded together with a strong, waterproof, woodworking adhesive. Liberally coat both rough surfaces, lay one panel face down on a flat clean surface and press the other panel firmly onto it so that the edges are flush. Using heavy weights on spare lumber, the two panels should be pressed together for 24 hours.

Marking out

When the glue has dried, mark out the finished panel for the pieces for the table top and legs. The dimensions of these three pieces are given in Figs. 1 and 2. Now mark out the patterns for the top and legs using Figs. 1 and 2 as a guide. To make the scalloped edge of the table top, first draw a circle on the panel using a pencil on a string which is pinned to the center of the table top, then, using the same equipment, make four equal and equidistant arcs around the circle. When marking out the patterns for the legs ensure that the housing marked on each panel are at opposite sides of the leg. Also note that only one leg is fitted with the female parts of the leg-fixing door bolt and that this leg must have the housing slot cut from the top, long, straight edge.

Cutting out and assembly

Cut out the parts with a jig saw or a hand keyhole-type saw. When cutting any curved lines do not work exactly to the mark but leave a small margin which can be sanded down later. The six leg location blocks are made from offcuts.

Clean up the edges of the cut panels, using medium and then fine sandpaper. Fix the leg locating blocks to the underside of the table top using Fig. 1 as a guide. To ensure a strong bond, sandpaper away the smooth hardboard face where the blocks are located.

Fix the female part of the bolts into the leg slots using an epoxy adhesive, then use this leg member to mark the location of the bolts on the underside of the table top. Glue the bolts in position, with epoxy adhesive, first roughening the joining surfaces to ensure a good grip.

Finishing off

Using fine sandpaper, carefully smooth the completed structure and add the finish desired. If you decide to paint the table, first apply an undercoat then two coats of high gloss polyurethane.

The completed table is now ready for use and once you have seen the attractive results you can obtain in hardboard, you will be prompted to make other units in this versatile and inexpensive material.

Cutting list

Hardboard	Standard	Metric
2 $\frac{1}{8}$in panels	24in x 48in	600mm x 1200mm

When glued together these panels are cut to give: 2 leg members, 1 table top and 6 leg locating blocks to the sizes shown in the figures.
You will also need:
2 small flat door bolts. Woodworking adhesive. Medium and fine sandpaper. Jig saw or keyhole-type saw. Paint or self-adhesive plastic laminate.

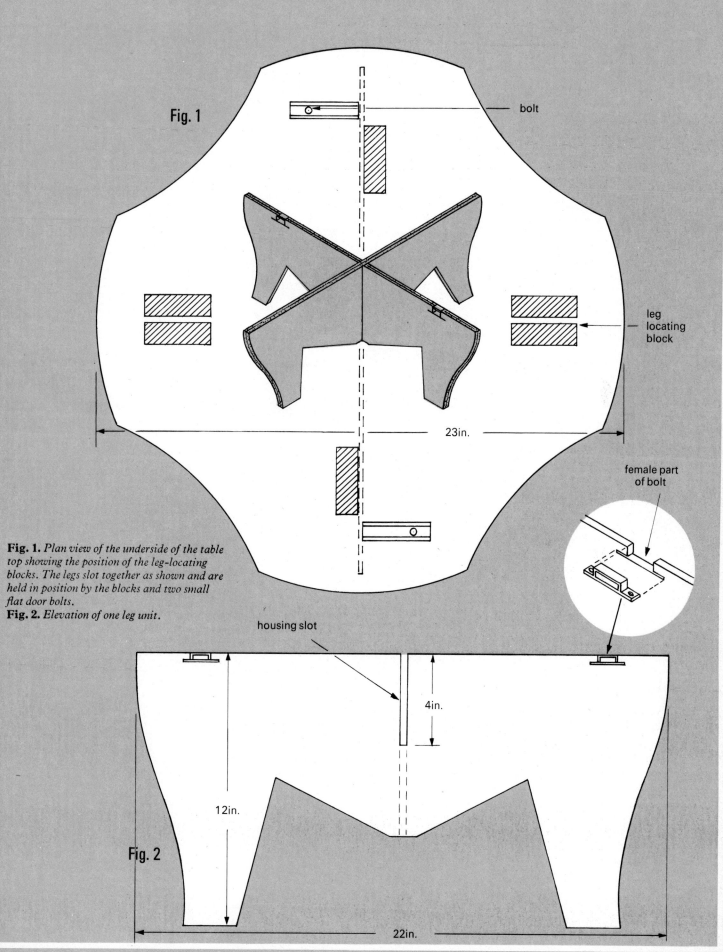

Fig. 1

bolt

leg
locating
block

Fig. 1. *Plan view of the underside of the table top showing the position of the leg-locating blocks. The legs slot together as shown and are held in position by the blocks and two small flat door bolts.*
Fig. 2. *Elevation of one leg unit.*

23in.

female part
of bolt

housing slot

4in.

12in.

Fig. 2

22in.

Adjustable bookrack

This adjustable bookrack helps solve what is often one of the trick-iest storage problems in the home – where to put the books that a family accumulates. The bookrack can be placed on any convenient surface and will keep your books upright in a neat row – which looks far better than books leaning at all angles in open shelves.

The bookrack consists of a base and two book ends which slide in a groove in the base panel. The book ends are designed to 'lock' when pushed near their top end but slide easily when pushed near the base. The pressure of books in the rack will cause the book ends to lock – so books can't slide about and fall over.

General construction

The base of the bookrack consists of two pieces of lumber, cut to the dimensions shown in Fig. 1. These are screwed to three legs so that their long sides are parallel and there is a gap of $\frac{3}{4}$in (↑9mm) between them.

Each book end is made of a piece of lumber, rounded at the top, which runs at right angles to the base in the finished construction. These strips are screwed to triangular pieces which are positioned on the outer surfaces of the book ends, along their vertical center line. The triangu-lar pieces extend below the groove in the base in the finished construction and plastic-covered steel pins are positioned at their bottom to allow the book ends to slide along the groove.

Materials

The bookrack shown in the photograph is made from a teak pattern, pre-finished, plastic-coated chipboard material. If you cut this material, as you must for this project, the exposed edges should be covered with matching edging strip.

The bookrack can also be built out of solid wood, or plywood. You can also use wood-veneered chipboard, though here again you will need to apply matching edging strip to exposed edges.

If you choose any of the chipboard-based materials you should glue fiber screw plugs into all holes. This makes for greater holding power.

The base

The base consists of two 30in x 3$\frac{3}{4}$in (762mm x 95mm) boards which are laid parallel to each other, with a $\frac{3}{4}$in (19mm) gap between their long edges.

Three wooden legs, screwed to the base members, hold them together.

Cut the two base members to size and apply edging strip to all exposed edges. Both wood veneer and plastic laminate edging strip can be purchased in rolls – use a contact adhesive to glue plastic edging strip in place and a white wood glue for wood veneer edging strip. If you use contact adhesive, wipe excess from the base members with a damp cloth. You can leave any excess blobs of contact adhesive to set – these can then be lifted from the base members with a handyman's knive.

Cut the three wooden legs to the shape and dimensions shown in Fig. 1. These should be shaped from a piece of material that matches the wood used for the bookrack – in the rack shown in the photograph the teak pattern chip-board is matched by legs of solid teak. Lay the two base members on a flat surface with a $\frac{3}{4}$in (19mm) thick piece of waste lumber between them. This is to maintain an equal slot right along the base. Mark the position of the legs on the base. Drill holes through the legs for 1½in No. 6 countersunk screws, four for each leg. Drill holes in the base members for fiber wood plugs suitable for this type of screw. Be careful not to drill right through the base members – a drill stop or a piece of colored adhesive tape wrapped around the drill bit will prevent this.

The book ends

The book ends have a T-shaped cross-section. The strips that run at right angles to the base are screwed to triangular pieces of wood. These triangular pieces protrude through the slot in the base and are held in place with plastic-covered steel pins or nails.

Cut the book-end components to the shape and dimensions given in Fig. 1. The triangular components can be cut from one piece of rectangular lumber – simply mark one of the diagonals and cut down it. Cut the housing in the long, straight side of the triangular pieces.

Apply edging strip to all exposed edges – except, of course, the sides of the housing in the triangular pieces. Now lay the triangular pieces on a flat surface and mark on them the positions of the plastic-covered steel pins. These are shown in Fig. 1. If you have altered the thickness of the material used for the base, you will have to adjust the positions of the pins.

The steel pins are cut from 3in (75mm) round nails. Each pin is 1⅛in (28mm) long. Drill holes for the pins at the marked points. These holes should provide what is known as an 'interference' fit – this means that the pins can be knocked in tightly so that they will not fall out.

The ends of the pins are covered with neoprene or plastic tubing. This is to protect the surface of the base from scratches as the book ends slide along. This tubing is available from model makers' stores, hardware and car accessory dealers. If you find this difficult, the pins can be painted to match the wood, or you can use larger dkameter wooden dowels.

Now assemble the ends, screwing through the book ends into the face of the housing in the triangular pieces. Use fiber screw plugs in the triangular pieces to give a secure fixing. 1½in (38mm) No. 6 countersunk wood screws are suitable.

Finishing

If you use plastic-laminated chipboard for the bookrack, all you have to do to finish the components is to lift any dried blobs of excess adhesive from the components with a sharp handyman's knife. Then dust down the components.

For plywood, rub down the lumber with a fine sandpaper and apply a coat of clear varnish.

When this dries, rub it down with steel wool. The finish for hardwood will depend on the type of lumber you use. Teak, for example, should be sandpapered to a smooth finish and then coated with mineral spirits blended 50/50 with a clear matte polyurethane varnish. This is then rubbed down with sandpaper, a second coat of the same mixture applied and rubbed down with steel wool when dry. The surfaces are then cleaned well with mineral spirits and left overnight. The final step is to apply teak oil sparingly.

Assembly

Now try the book ends in the base. Slide the ends in place from one end of the base. The ends should slide easily when pushed at the base but lock if pushed near the top – so that books leaning over in the rack can't push the ends apart. If the book ends do not lock as required, roughen the surfaces around the slot on the underside of the base. This will prevent the book ends sliding quite so freely.

Once you have a satisfactory fit, drill for and fix a ½in (13mm) No. 4 round-headed wood screw in the end legs between the sides of the slot. This stops the book ends sliding off the base completely.

All you need do now is put the bookrack in a convenient place and fill it with books.

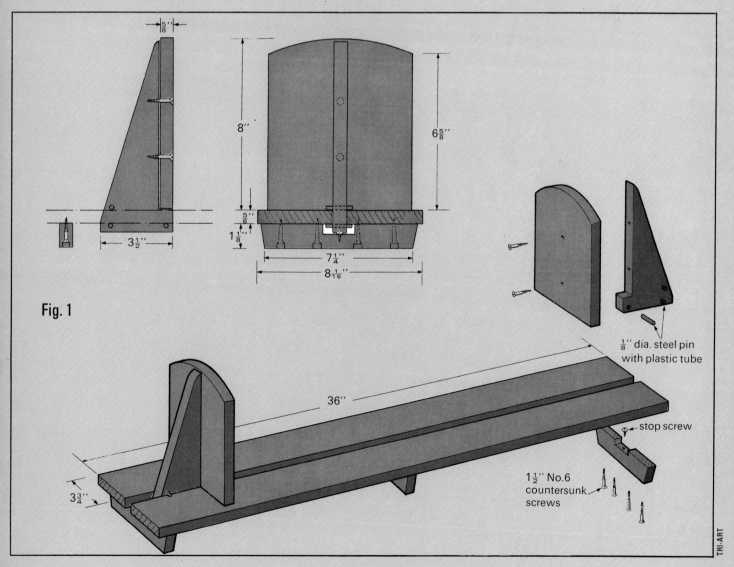

Fig. 1

⅛'' dia. steel pin with plastic tube

stop screw

1½'' No.6 countersunk screws

TRI-ART

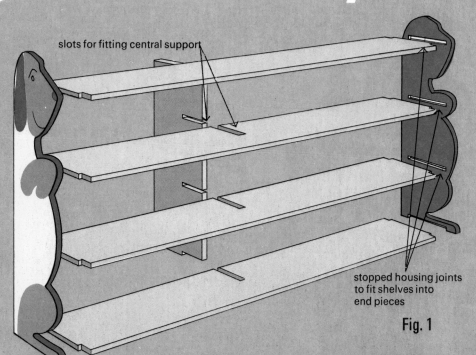

slots for fitting central support

stopped housing joints
to fit shelves into
end pieces

Fig. 1

A 'doggy' bookcase

Children like furniture that they feel has been specially made for them. Mass-produced children's furniture so often lacks the personal touch that the individual child cherishes. An attractively original idea, and one which is ideal for a nursery or children's bedroom is this Doggy Bookcase. Use the idea to give your children's bedroom or playroom a highly novel piece of furniture.

The idea of this bookcase is that the end supports for the shelves are cut into the shape of a dog and painted with bright and cheerful colors. For the children the end supports can be cut and painted to represent almost any animal – a rabbit, a bear, a cat or even a chimpanzee.

If you are not very skilled at drawing why not cut the picture from one of those large and colorful animal posters that are specially designed for children.

The construction of the bookcase is very simple. It's best to begin by cutting the ends. Cut both ends together. This will ensure that an identical shape will be achieved. Because of the depth of the bookcase each end will need to be made of two 9in (225mm) planks, which have to be joined together before proceeding to cut the shape of the dog. To join the planks just plane the edges to be fixed together square. Having done this glue the planks, planed edge to planed edge, with a wood adhesive. Hold the planks in place with sash clamps. Before the adhesive sets knock the planks level along the join with a hammer – using a block of waste wood to avoid damaging the planks' surface.

Left. The finished bookcase looks most attractive in a playroom—and with a little imagination can be adapted for adult use.

Cutting out the end

Once you are sure the adhesive has set you can begin to cut out the dog. Release the sash clamps and lay one of the end pieces on a bench. Draw the outline of the dog carefully, using a wax crayon. Wax crayons are easier to use on wood than a pencil and the line drawn will be more clearly visible. Having drawn the dog lay the end piece on top of the other piece and hold them firmly in place with 'C' clamps. The shape of the dog should be cut with a coping saw – or, if you have one – a jig saw. Hold the ends firmly against the edge of the bench with a vise with the drawn outline of the dog facing you. Cut the two end pieces carefully around the outline.

Construction

The shelves of the bookcase are made in the same way as the end pieces, i.e. by joining two 9in planks edge to edge with each other. Joining the shelves to the end pieces is done by means of stopped housing joints as shown in Fig. 1. Slots are cut into the end pieces, to a depth of approximately half the thickness of the wood, to take the shelf ends. The joints are secured with a good woodworking adhesive and slim nails skew-nailed through the bottoms of the shelves, upward into the end pieces.

Fitting the central support of the bookcase is a very simple matter. Cut slots into the support plank as shown in Fig. 1. These should be cut to half the width of the plank. Corresponding slots should be cut in the shelves, using direct marking (see Fig. 1). (Or you may prefer to cut both sets of slots before you begin construction.) You then slot in the support, securing the joints with wood adhesive.

The doggy bookcase pictured here is really intended to hold children's toys. If you intend your bookcase to hold books you will need to install additional support for a bookcase of this length. If you do not do this the shelves will not stand the weight. This will mean adding extra supports in the same way as the central support shown in this example.

The design of the doggy bookcase lends itself to almost infinite versatility. You don't have to restrict yourself to making a bookcase or a place to put toys. The idea can be adapted to an adult environment very easily. Why not make a wall unit by using the same method of construction? The end pieces can be decorated with any illustration to suit the decor of your living room, study or bedroom. A standing unit can accomodate a great many household items – television, radio and stereo set as well as books will find a convenient home on the shelves.

If you don't feel able to draw an illustration on the end pieces yourself there are a vast choice of posters available from which you could take a tracing. In the case of a high wall unit two or more posters can be combined, the same posters for each end, to achieve a pleasing and original design. You could either cut the silhouettes of the posters out in the same way as the shape of the dog or, if you prefer, simplify the design by leaving the posters as they are. This treatment is most suitable for posters with no dominant image to cut out.

A magazine rack

Magazine racks can be as attractive as they are functional. This simple design, which can be made from any wood and heavy cloth, is ideal for storing magazines and papers and, with only a few modifications, could hold anything from records to knitting. The materials you use can be chosen to complement any decor or color scheme, but the real attraction of this piece is its low price and ease of construction.

Make sure before you start that you have all the tools and materials shown in the cutting list. Decide what sort of wood you want to use, and how you are going to treat it. If you decide on pine it may be left untreated or painted. Other woods can be varnished. The choice of suitable cloth is wide, although it should be heavy enough to hang properly and be printed or dyed on both sides. Burlap or canvas go particularly well with natural or painted pine. The three supporting rods can be of wood or metal — the type of metal rod used for bathroom towel racks is suitable. When buying the spring clips, you will find household utility clips are the most readily available. Spring-based and used for storing mops, brooms, etc., they come in varying sizes and strengths.

Preparations

Care must be taken when measuring and marking out. 'Measure twice, cut once' saves time and waste. This is particularly important when you are building any item with legs, especially a narrow unit like this. You must make sure that the legs are exactly equal in length. When you are satisfied with the measuring, cut all pieces to the sizes given in the cutting list and sand them smooth with fine sandpaper. You will find it easier to produce a good finish at this stage rather than when the frame is completed.

Assembling the frame

Assembling is easy provided you have cut and sanded the pieces correctly so that their edges are flat and smooth. Lay two of the legs on a flat surface and glue one of the end panels across them so that the top of the end panel is flush with the top of the legs. When the panel is properly positioned, secure it with nails, using the fine punch to sink their heads below surface. Now repeat with the other two legs. Nail and glue the handles in position. These lie across the leg tops, flush with the end panel on one side and overhanging the tops of the legs at the other side.

Now nail and glue the rod stop battening inside each of the two end panels. These must be flush with the bottom of each panel.

To fix the side members to the end frames, drill two screw holes 1in inward from both ends of each side member, and countersink to accommodate the screwheads. Lay one side member across the two frames, using Fig. 2 as a guide. The side members are positioned so that the top screw holes are 3½in from the top surfaces of the handles. The ends of the side panels must be flush with the overhanging

Fig. 1. A detail of one end of the magazine rack showing how the supporting rods clip on to the frame. This attachment allows you to clean the material easily. Simply unclip the rods and pull them through the folds.
Fig. 2. *An exploded diagram of the rack. Its ease of construction is matched by its neatness and utility. The unit can be painted or varnished to match your decor.*

edges of the handles immediately above. Repeat on the other side with the other panel, and screw into position. If you are using 'screw-cap' screws fit the plastic heads onto the screws. You have only to fit the six spring clips into position to complete the frame. These are fastened, three along each side as shown in Fig. 1. When you come to clipping in the rods you may find it necessary to cut or file them to size.

Test the rack for wobble by standing it on a flat surface. If any of the legs are of unequal length, place waste pieces of wood under them until the frame stands level. Take a waste block of wood measuring about 3in x 2in x ½in and drill a hole through the ½in edge just big enough to tightly hold a pencil. Push the pencil through so that about 1in protrudes, and lay the block flat on the surface so the pencil is parallel to the floor. Draw a line around the bottom of each leg and very carefully cut through the legs, around these lines, using a fine saw.

Finishing the frame

The magazine rack frame is now complete, but before you begin painting or varnishing, give it a really professional finish by filling all holes caused by the nails with a wood filler. When the surfaces are flat, paint or varnish the frame in the colors of your choice.

To get the best results when painting the rack you should start with a coat of primer, followed by the undercoat and then the top coat. If you use polyurethane varnish, use three coats, rubbing each with sandpaper when dry before applying subsequent coats.

Fixing the cloth

Turn all the edges of the cloth making a ½in hem all around. If you are using a heavy cloth such as canvas you will probably find it easier to glue the hems before stitching together. The rods must fit into folds sewn into the cloth as shown in Fig. 2. Make three folds, one at each short side of the cloth and one in the middle allowing 1½in for each fold. The rods are pushed through the folds and clipped into place.

Fig. 2

- end handle
- end panel
- rod stop battening
- side member
- rod
- spring clips
- 1 in. screws with plastic screw caps
- cloth
- leg

Cutting list

Solid wood	Standard	Metric
4 legs	17½ x 1¼ x 1¼	452 x 31 x 31
2 end panels	8½ x 5 x ½	216 x 127 x 13
2 handles	8½ x 2 x ½	216 x 51 x 13
2 rod stops	8½ x 1½ x ½	216 x 38 x 13
2 side members	24 x 3 x ½	610 x 76 x 13
Metal or dowelling		
3 rods	20 (½ diam.)	508 (13)
Cloth	48 x 18½	1219 x 470

You will also require: 6 spring clips such as household utility clips used for door-storage, to take the ½in rods. Eight 1in screws. About 40 1in nails. Hammer. Tenon saw. Fine punch for nails. Fine sandpaper. Paint or varnish.

All measurements are exact — allow 10% for waste when ordering. Standard measurements in inches. Metric measurements in millimeters.

TRI-ART

TRANSWORLD

Cushions for furniture

Tables, chairs, beds and playthings – cover blocks of foam with hard-wearing covers and you have cushions that can turn into virtually any kind of furniture your children need. Compare the variety of uses – and the cost – with that of more conventional children's furniture and you'll be surprised at what you gain – and save. Floor cushions are so good an idea you may even find yourself making up some for your own lounging area.

Above. *If your instinct leads you to choosing bright, primary colors for the covers, beware— these will show every mark (including muddy footprints). Play safe with dark colors.*

it is worth bearing in mind the width of the fabric you are using for the cover.

For example, if you are making it by the boxed method, it is simplest and most economical if you can cut the fabric in half lengthwise and use one piece for the top and the other for the bottom.

Making the cover

This sort of cushion is seen from all sides and so the most logical way to use the fabric – even if it is patterned – is with the selvage threads running along the length of the pad. This way you should not need any joins on the main panels. However, if you are making the cover by the boxed method (see below), the pattern on the box strips must run from the top of the cushion to the bottom when in position, rather than on its side around the edge, so you may

If you have an old foam mattress which is in reaonable condition – perhaps after buying a new mattress for your own bed – this is ideal for making floor cushions. You can cut it to the size and shape you want with a fine-toothed hacksaw, a really sharp, long cook's knife or an electric carving knife.

If you have to buy the foam, do choose one with a high density, with a minimum of 1·5lb per

cu ft – anything lower than this will not be strong enough. The density of some types of foam does not effect the feel of it, and from a large stockist you can buy a variety of thicknesses in a variety of 'feels'. For this purpose, a fairly hard foam between 4–6in deep is usually best, particularly if the cushions will also be slept on. The other measurements of the pad are obviously up to you but, when you are deciding, have to join fabric here.

If the foam is latex, it is worth making a non-removable inner lining cover from calico. This will act as a barrier for the fragments of foam which tend to work loose, and cling to the cover fabric, which is unsightly.

Make the inner cover by the second method given below, and finish the opening with over-sewing, rather than a zipper because this will be flatter and cheaper.

A tailored cover for a foam pad with square sides can be made by one of two methods. The first method should be used if you want a piped edge, if you are using a patterned fabric with a one-way design (see above), or if the pad is an irregular shape.

The cover should fit the pad tightly and smoothly, so if you cut it slightly smaller than the foam this will be permanently under compression and stretch the cover into clean lines without wrinkles.

Boxed method

Add $\frac{3}{4}$in to the length and width of the pad

Below. *Use a stout furnishing fabric or a stretch dress jersey for the covers, because either of these will stand up to the rigors of a floor cushion.*

and cut two rectangles of fabric, on the straight grain, to this size. For the box stripes, which are inserted between the main sections, cut three strips $\frac{3}{4}$in wider than the depth of the cushion, and long enough to fit the front and two sides plus $\frac{3}{4}$in. Join the side strips to each side of the main strip along the short edges, tacking $\frac{1}{2}$in turnings. Taper the stitching into the corners $\frac{1}{2}$in from the beginning and end of each seam.

Cut another strip 1in wider than the others and long enough to fit the back of the cushion, plus $\frac{3}{4}$in for turnings. Cut this strip in half lengthwise and re-join it for $\frac{3}{4}$in at each end taking $\frac{1}{2}$in turnings. Insert a zipper into the remaining opening. Stitch the short ends of this strip to the short ends of the other one, take $\frac{1}{2}$in turnings and taper the stitching as before.

If you are having piping, attach this around both edges of the now circular strip, taking $\frac{1}{2}$in turnings. Clip the piping casing fabric in line with the joining seams of the strip.

With the wrong side of the strip facing out and the top of the pattern towards the top, fit the panel for the top of the cushion on to the top edge of the strip, matching the corners to the seams. Stitch in position and overcast the edges of the fabric which otherwise is likely to fray. The tapered seams of the strip will open out as you do this, so there is no need to clip into the

corners. Press carefully.

Still with the wrong side fabric out, turn the strip so that the open end is facing up. Fit the fabric for the bottom of the cushion to this side, matching the corners to the seams as before. Press and turn right-side out.

Two-panel method

Double the depth measurement of the pad, add this to both the length and width, and add on $\frac{3}{4}$in each way for the turnings. Cut a piece of fabric on the straight grain to this size.

Measure in from the corners in both directions the depth of the pad, plus $\frac{1}{2}$in and mark. Fold over the adjacent sides at each corner, matching the marks, to make a dart, and stitch up from the marks to the fold on the straight grain of the fabric. Trim off the excess fabric to within $\frac{1}{4}$in of the stitching.

Cut a second piece of fabric to the size of the bottom of the pad, plus $\frac{3}{4}$in each way for turnings. With the wrong side of the fabric facing outward on both sections, fit the smaller piece to the open side of the other piece, matching the corners to the darts. Stitch on three sides, taking $\frac{1}{2}$in turnings and clipping them where necessary on the main section for a smooth finish. Press and turn right side out. Finish the opening with a zipper.

things to do in a day

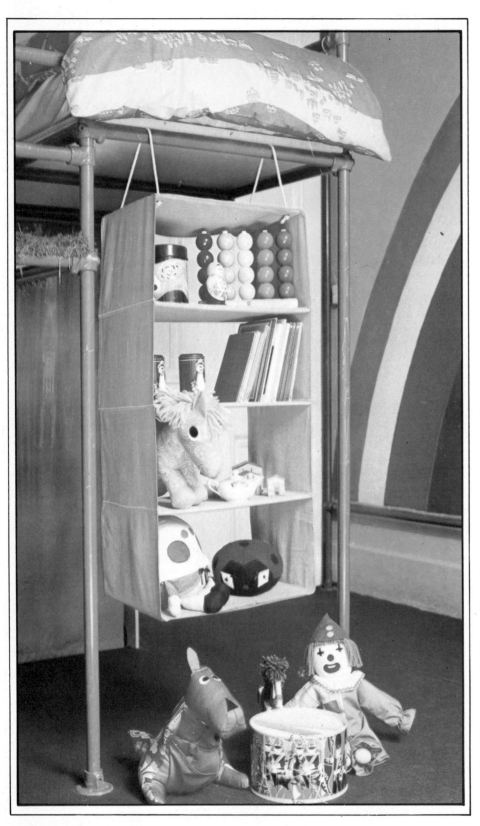

The shelves of the hanging unit are made from doubled heavy-duty canvas which forms pockets into which pieces of plywood are inserted for extra support.

Fabric required
3 yards (2·7 5metres) heavy-duty canvas. 36 inches (91cm) wide

You will also need
Five pieces of $\frac{1}{4}$ inch (0·6cm) plywood $17\frac{3}{4}$ inches (45cm) x $11\frac{3}{4}$ inches (30cm)
Strong sewing thread to match the canvas
Heavy machine needle
1 yard (90cm) rope $\frac{1}{4}$ inch (0·6cm) thick
Hand drill
Drill bit $\frac{3}{8}$ inch (1cm) diameter
Four eyelets $\frac{3}{8}$ inch (1cm) diameter
Hooks for hanging the shelves

Cutting out the canvas
Cut out the canvas pieces as shown in the cutting chart.

Making up
1 Fold the main panel in half across the width and mark the fold line with a basting stitch to indicate the centre top of the unit.
2 Join the short ends of the panel, with right sides together, taking $\frac{1}{2}$ inch (1·3cm) turnings.

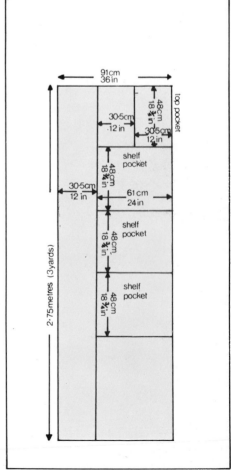

Hang it
. . . anywhere you need an extra shelf or two. These attractive shelves are space-savers and simple to make.

Machine stitch using strong thread and a heavy needle.

3 Press the turnings open and machine stitch them down to the wrong side of the panel.

4 Make a narrow hem along the raw edge of the panel. If you have a zig-zag machine this can be done with a single line of stitching closely zig-zag stitched into place.

5 Fold the piece for the top pocket in half across the width. Crease lightly.

6 Open it out and make a narrow hem along one of the longer sides. Turn under a $\frac{3}{8}$ inch (1cm) hem on the wrong side along the remaining three sides.

7 Place the pocket, wrong side down, on the wrong side of the main panel so that the crease line marking the centre of the pocket falls over the basted line at the top of the panel exactly.

8 Measure 2 inches (5cm) diagonally from the corners of the pocket and make tailor's tacks through both layers of canvas. Cut through the tacks and open out the layers. Make eyelet holes in the position of the tacks at each corner in both pieces of canvas.

9 Replace the pocket, matching the holes. Leaving the side with the narrow hem open, pin and machine stitch the remaining sides of the pocket to the main panel along the folds of the turnings. Work a second line of machine stitching $\frac{1}{4}$ inch (0·6cm) away from the first line.

10 Fold the piece for the bottom pocket in half across the width. Crease lightly.

11 Open it out and make a narrow hem along one of the longer sides. Turn under a $\frac{3}{8}$ inch (1cm) hem on the wrong side along the remaining three sides.

12 Place the pocket, wrong side down, on the wrong side of the main panel so that the center crease line falls exactly over the seam line at the bottom of the panel and the hem of the pocket is on the same side as the opening of the top pocket. Machine stitch the pocket to the main panel along the other three sides.

Attaching the shelves

1 Make narrow hems along the short raw edges of the three remaining pocket pieces. Fold the pockets in half across the width with the right side out and press.

2 Measure down the required depth of the shelf from the top pocket on each side of the main panel and mark.

3 Keeping the opening of the pocket to the same side as the others and with turnings up, pin the doubled short sides of the pocket to the main strip along the marks indicated, taking $\frac{1}{2}$ inch (1·3cm) turnings. Machine stitch twice.

4 Attach the other shelves in the same way, ensuring that the distance between them on each side of the main panel is the same.

Strengthening the shelves

1 To cover the raw edges of the shelves where they are stitched to the main panel, cut six strips, $1\frac{1}{2}$ inches (4cm) x $12\frac{1}{2}$ inches (32cm) from the leftover canvas. Turn under a narrow hem on the wrong side of each side of the strips and press.

2 Place each strip over the raw edges of a seam joining the pockets to the main panel so that the lower edge of the strip is level with the stitch line. Pin in position and machine stitch around all sides. Repeat this procedure with each of the other seams.

3 Insert the pieces of plywood into the shelves.

4 Insert the plywood into the pocket at the top of unit and mark the positions of the eyelet holes in pencil. Take out the wood and drill holes in each position. Replace the wood so that the holes correspond with the eyelets.

5 Cut the rope in half and tie a double knot at one end of each half. Insert the other end of one of the pieces up through the eyelet hole at the front of the unit and then down through the hole at the back on the same side. Tie a knot underneath. Repeat this with the other piece of rope on the opposite side.

6 Attach hooks in the required place, adjust the rope to the desired length and hang in position on the hooks, or hang the unit over a horizontal rod as pictured.

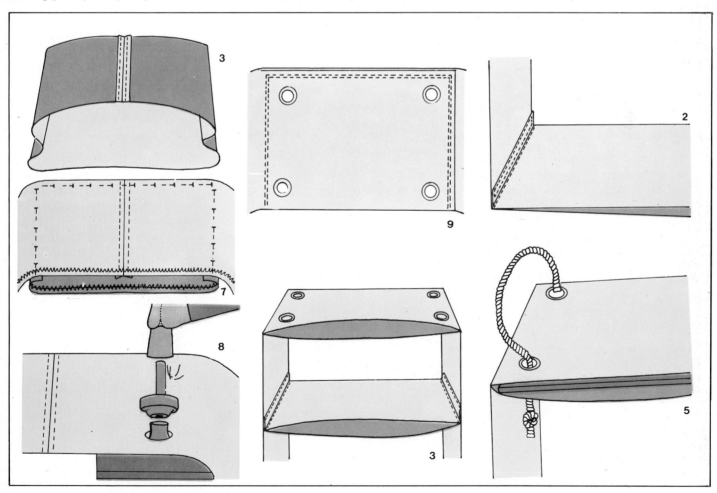

The dimensions of the lamp may be altered to your particular specifications, depending where you want to put it. The decorative tiles give an interesting finish to the unit and can be obtained in a wide variety of designs and colors. Complete the stand before choosing the shade; your choice should complement the simple lines of the stand.

Preparation

Make sure you have all the necessary tools and materials before measuring your wood to the sizes given in the cutting list. Mark out the correct panel sizes and cut them carefully so that each edge is flat. Because each edge must lie flush with a plane surface it is important that any irregularities are sanded out. Use a fine sandpaper to smooth all the surfaces.

Assembling the stand

Assembly is simple. Begin by taking the two large panels and mark out a line $\frac{1}{2}$in (13mm) in from each long edge. This measurement represents the amount by which the shorter panels are recessed. On the short sides of the large panels mark a line $\frac{3}{4}$in (18mm) from each edge — the distance by which the larger panels overlap the smaller.

Apply glue to the long edges of the smaller panels and to a $\frac{1}{2}$in strip inside the line drawn on the larger panel. Fix the smaller panel between the larger, making sure the outer surface is recessed to the marks, and that the short edges are overlapped by the large panels to the correct distance. Allow the glue to dry, then use $1\frac{1}{4}$in (32mm) slim nails to secure the panels.

The basic structure of the sides is now complete. To fix the top and bottom, first drill a $\frac{1}{2}$in (13mm) diameter hole in the center of both panels. These holes take the flex. Glue and nail one of these panels to the top of the recessed sides so the two short edges are flush with the edges of the larger side panels. Now take the tubing, apply a smear of glue on the last $\frac{1}{2}$in of each end, and push it through the hole in the top so the edge of the tube is just below the panel surface. Glue and nail the bottom panel to the side panels first checking it is flush and that the tubing is properly housed in the center hole. The tubing acts as a conduit for the flex and allows you to change the lamp holder or flex without dismantling the top and bottom panels. When you have done this add the feet to the base.

Gluing the tiles

The tiles are fixed to the recessed sides with a strong ceramic adhesive. Make sure both gluing surfaces are clean and apply a liberal amount of adhesive to the surface of the panel and the back of each tile. Press the tiles into position — there should be an equal gap between

Versatile lamp-base

This elegant table lamp in a modern design is pleasingly different. Too often a contemporary piece of furniture is marred by an old-fashioned table lamp — and old wine bottles are not always the answer! The uncluttered lines of this lamp will enhance any modern piece of furniture and it is very easy to make.

each tile and between the tile and side panel – and allow the adhesive to set. When the adhesive has set, fill the spaces between the tiles – the grouts – with a grouting compound for that purpose, so that each tile stands out from the surface about $\frac{1}{8}$in (3mm).

Fixing the lamp holder

Take the threaded brass ring, center it over the hole in the top panel and screw it into place using three $\frac{5}{8}$in (16mm) screws. Connect the flex to the lamp holder, thread it through the tubing and screw the socket into place on the brass base. The assembly of the lamp standard is now complete.

Painting the lamp

Before you can get a glossy painted finish there are certain rules to be observed. If there are any scratches or grooves in the panels these must be sanded out. Deeper grooves should be filled with wood filler. Apply an even undercoat and when this has dried use two coats of polyurethane gloss paint to give a fine finish. Take extra care when painting the butt joints to fill any gaps there may be. A small fine brush should be used for these joints and for painting the areas around the tiles.

Choosing a shade

Choose a shade which is in proportion with the stand. A simple design is best, because it will not clash with or detract from the elegant lines of the stand and allows the tiles to show to their greatest effect.

Below. *An exploded view of the top half of the base. Ceramic tiles are fixed to the sides, or you could use something else, such as polished wood panels, vinyl tiles, cork, fabric or even wallpaper.*

Cutting list

$\frac{1}{2}$in Birch plywood	inches	millimeters
2 side panels	$14\frac{3}{8} \times 5\frac{1}{2}$	367 x 139
2 side panels	$13 \times 4\frac{1}{2}$	330 x 114
1 top panel	$5\frac{1}{2} \times 4\frac{1}{2}$	139 x 114
1 bottom panel	$5\frac{1}{2} \times 4\frac{1}{2}$	139 x 114

You will also need:
6 ceramic tiles
Surface fitting lamp holder with threaded brass base.
$13\frac{3}{4}$in length of tubing $\frac{1}{2}$in external diameter and of an internal diameter to take the flex.
Ceramic adhesive capable of bonding wood to tile.
Filling or grouting compound.
Wood adhesive.
50 $1\frac{1}{4}$in panel pins. Three $\frac{5}{8}$in brass screws.
Rip saw, hammer, small screwdriver.
Undercoat and polyurethane gloss.
Four rubber-headed nails for feet.

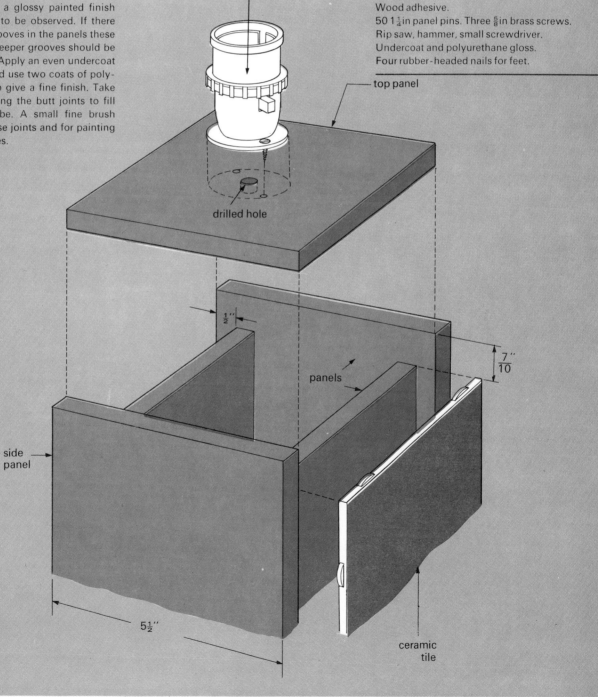

lamp holder

top panel

drilled hole

$\frac{1}{2}$"

panels

$\frac{7}{10}$"

side panel

$5\frac{1}{2}$"

ceramic tile

things to do in a day

length that suits its location. Make sure, when buying the lumber, that it is well seasoned — unseasoned lumber may twist and warp out of shape in time.

Each side of the rack is fitted with 5in (125mm) aluminium hat and coat hooks — the number you use depends on the length of rack you want.

A 1in (25mm) metal screw eye is fixed into the end grain of the rack at the top.

This connects to a metal hook which is fixed either to a ceiling joist or the underside of a closet shelf.

Locating the rack

The rack may be hung from the ceiling in any suitable corner or in a closet. Fixing the rack in a closet, with the top hook screwed into one of the shelves may present a problem — the shelf may not be thick enough to give an adequate fixing to the hook. You can overcome this by screwing a wooden batten to the underside of the shelf. This will also help prevent any tendency for the shelf to sag under the weight of the rack and coats.

To hang the rack from the ceiling, the top hook must be screwed into a ceiling joist — plaster will not provide an adequate fixing.

Locating a suitable joist should present few problems. You can usually locate joists by tapping the ceiling with your knuckles and listening for the deader sound — this will be underneath a joist.

If you can't find a joist in this way though, a few test bores into the ceiling with a hand drill fitted with a small-diameter drill bit will do the job. Alternatively, if you have access to the area above the joists — by means of a loft above the top-floor rooms, for example — you can drill a small hole down each side of one joist, through the ceiling. Then, when you come to hang the rack, simply position the top fixing hook between these holes. The guide holes are made good later.

Hanging the rack from the ceiling may mean that the top coat hooks will be well out of reach of an average size person. One way of overcoming this is to suspend the rack from a short length of cable — metal Bowden cable is the best choice but you could use nylon rope, providing it is fully stretched before you hang the rack from it. If you do suspend the rack from cable, substitute the top fixing hook in the end grain of the wood for a metal screw eye the same size as that used for the ceiling or shelf fixing.

Hanging storage rack

For the small home, or the crowded home, this hook-up storage rack is a valuable space saver that will fit — and look good — almost anywhere. The rack is particularly suited for hanging children's coats but you can use it for adults' coats or even as a novel shoetree.

The storage rack consists of a 2in x 2in (50mm x 50mm) length of lumber. A metal screw eye is fixed in the end grain at the top of the pole. This connects to a metal hook screwed into a ceiling joist or into the underside of a closet shelf.

Materials

The pole for the rack is a length of 2in x 2in (50mm x 50mm) planed lumber, cut to a

Cutting the lumber

You will have a rough idea of the height of rack you want when you buy the lumber. You can now cut the lumber exactly to length.

Make sure, when you do this, that the ends of

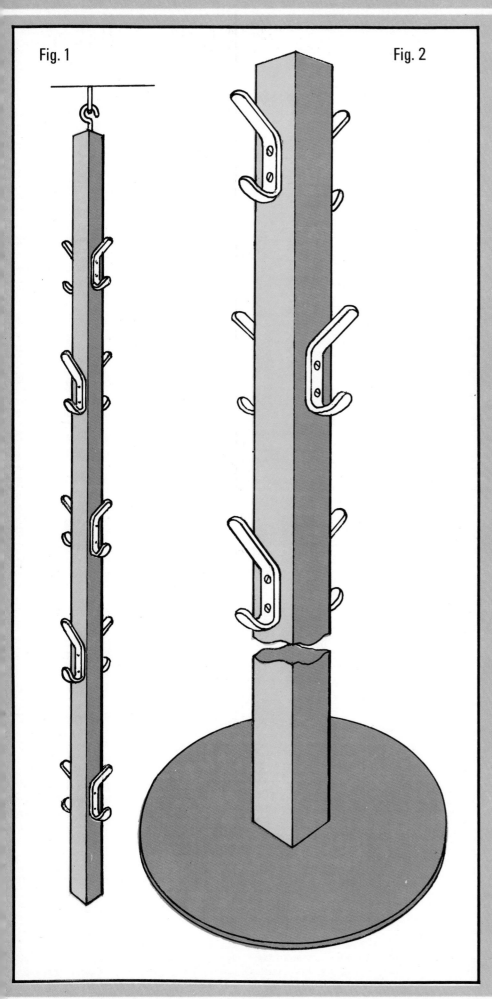

Fig. 1

Fig. 2

Fig. 1. *The hook-up storage rack, built to the specifications given here.*

Fig. 2. *A modified version of the storage rack. Here a base is screwed to the end grain at the bottom of the rack so that it will stand upright on the floor. The base can be cut from a sheet of ⅝in. (16mm) plywood, to a diameter of about 18in. (457mm). Draw the diameter with a large compass or with a piece of string attached to a pencil and a straight pin. Cut the plywood with a jigsaw. The base can be screwed to the end grain with two No. 6 2in. countersunk wood screws—but first glue fiber plugs into the end grain, to ensure that the screws do not pull out of the wood in time.*

the piece are cut square — an angled cut will look unsightly. To do this, lay a try square on the lumber at the required point. Score the lumber with a marking knife, running it along the blade of the square. Score all four surfaces. Then fill in the scored lines with a pencil, its point sharpened to a chisel edge. Cut through the marked lines.

Cut a slight bevel on the edges at both ends of the pole. Do this with a spokeshave. This is simply to eliminate sharp corners at the top and bottom of the rack.

Now drill a hole in the center of the end grain at the top of the rack.

Drill it oversize to allow for a standard plastic wall plug to be inserted. This is necessary to stop the screw thread of the hook pulling out of the end grain in time.

Locating the coat hooks

The rack shown in the photograph uses eighteen 5in coat hooks. Two of the sides have five hooks and the other two have four — these sets are placed on opposite surfaces.

In the original hook-up rack, the hooks are placed at 16in or 400mm centers. On the sides with five hooks, the first screw of the top hook is positioned $4\frac{1}{4}$in (106mm) down from the top of the rack. On the side's with four hooks. the first screw of the top hook is 1ft (305mm) down from the top. These positionings, like the length of the rack, are a matter of choice, though.

Mark the required positions of the hooks on the pole and drill for the screws — buy these when you get the hooks. ⅝in No. 5 countersunk wood screws are suitable.

Finishing

Planed lumber comes in what is called a 'pre-finished' finish — this means that the most you need do to produce a good surface is to plane it lightly with a finely set smoothing plane. You may be able to bring up the surface with sandpaper only.

You can either paint or varnish the rack. A polyurethane paint will produce a hardwearing surface. If you varnish the rack, use two or three coats of polyurethane varnish, rubbing down the surface of the rack with steel wool after each application.

When the paint or varnish has dried, fit the coat hooks and the screw eye at the top of the rack. Screw the eye fixing into the ceiling.

All you need do now is hang the rack and fill it with coats and shoes.

things to do in a day

lines. You can choose the tiles with which to decorate it to match your decor, or to add a splash of color to the hall area. Or you could use a material other than tiles, such as decorative self-adhesive papers or vinyl tiles.

Douglas fir plywood is the most suitable wood to use, as it takes a very smooth finish and is easy to work, although you could use almost any wood. With the range of tiles now avalable, you will have no difficulty in choosing the ideal pattern.

Preliminaries

Make sure you have all the necessary tools and materials before starting work. As with most apparently simple projects the standard of finish depends mainly on your accuracy in marking and cutting out. For this reason, take extra care over these, and when you have cut all the pieces out to the sizes given in the cutting list, check that their edges are smooth and plane.

Assembly

When you have cut out each piece, take the two large panels and mark out a line $\frac{1}{3}$in (8·5mm) in from each long edge. This measurement represents the amount by which the two shorter side panels are recessed. On the short sides of the large panels, mark a line 1$\frac{1}{4}$in (32mm) from each edge — the distance by which the larger panels overlap the smaller.

Apply glue to the long edges of the shorter side panels and to a $\frac{1}{2}$in (13mm) strip inside the line drawn on the longer side of the large side panels .Fix the smaller panels in position between the larger, making sure that the outer surfaces are recessed to the marks, and that their short edges are overlapped by the large panels to the correct distance. Allow the glue to dry, then use 1$\frac{1}{4}$in (32mm) slim nails to secure the structure.

Now add the bottom panels by gluing and screwing it to the recessed short edges of the smaller side panels. At the other end, fix the top edging into position. First take the 6$\frac{1}{4}$in x 1$\frac{1}{4}$in (159mm x 32mm) strips and glue them to the short edges of the recessed side panels, so that the outer long edge of each is flush with the long edges of the larger side panels. Then glue and nail the 5$\frac{3}{8}$in x $\frac{1}{4}$in (137mm x 6mm) strips between them as shown in the drawing opposite.

Gluing the tiles

The tiles are fixed to the recessed sides with a strong ceramic adhesive. Make sure that both surfaces are clean, and then apply a liberal amount of adhesive to the surface of the panel and the back of each tile. Press the tiles into position — there should be an equal gap between each tile and between tile and side panel — and allow the adhesive to set. When the adhesive has set, fill the spaces between the tiles — the

An umbrella stand

Brighten up your hallway with this easy to make umbrella stand. Large enough to hold several umbrellas, its simple lines, enhanced by decorative tiles, will enliven a part of the house which is so often neglected.

Despite the fact that the hall is the first part of your house that the visitor sees, much hall furniture remains drab and old-fashioned. A poor first impression is strengthened by the sight of a haphazard collection of coats and umbrellas with which many hallways are adorned.

This umbrella stand contributes toward a tidier and more attractive hall by providing a neat holder for umbrellas, and by its stylish modern grouts – with a grouting compound for that purpose so that the surface of each tile stands about $\frac{1}{8}$in (3mm) proud. Of course, if you decide to use some other material, you will have to use the appropriate gluing technique.

Painting the stand

Before you can get a glossy painted finish, there are certain rules to be observed. If there are any scratches or grooves in the panels these must be sanded out. Deeper grooves should be filled with wood filler. Apply an even undercoat and when this has dried, a coat of polyurethane gloss paint to give a fine finish. Take extra care when painting the butt joints to fill any gaps there may be. A small fine brush should be used for these joints and for painting the areas around the tiles.

If desired, you can drill a few holes in the base of the stand to allow any water that drips from an umbrella to drain away into a suitable receptacle.

CUTTING LIST

Douglas fir plywood $\frac{1}{2}$in (13mm)	Inches	Milli-meters
2 side panels	$20\frac{1}{2} \times 8$	520 x 203
2 side panels	$18\frac{1}{4} \times 6\frac{1}{4}$	464 x 159
1 bottom panel	$8 \times 6\frac{1}{4}$	203 x 159
2 top edging strips	$6\frac{1}{4} \times 1\frac{1}{4}$	159 x 32
2 top edging strips	$5\frac{3}{8} \times \frac{1}{4}$	137 x 6
You will also need:		
6 ceramic tiles	6×6	152 x 152

Ceramic adhesive capable of bonding wood to tile. Filling or grouting compound. Wood adhesive. 50 $1\frac{1}{4}$in (32mm) slim nails. 4 $1\frac{1}{4}$in (32mm) wood screws. Rip saw, hammer, undercoat and polyurethane gloss.

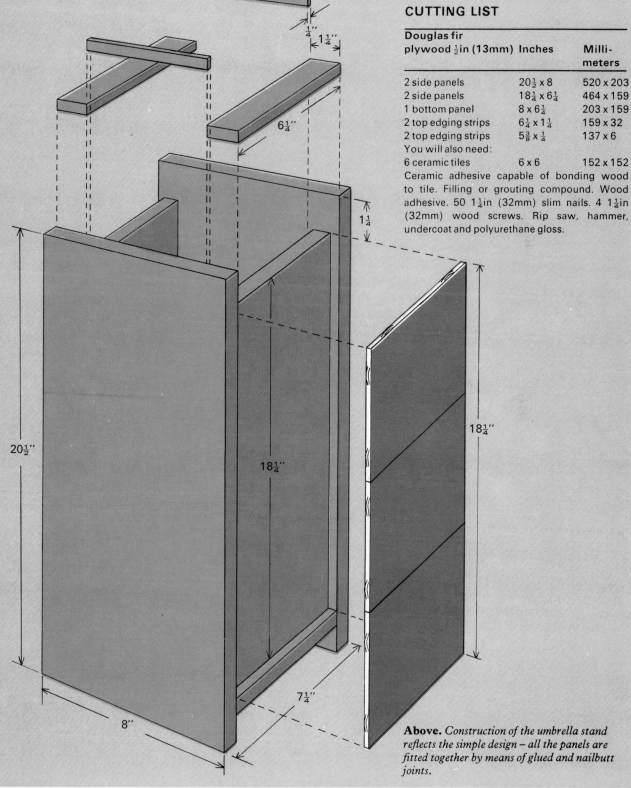

Above. *Construction of the umbrella stand reflects the simple design – all the panels are fitted together by means of glued and nailbutt joints.*

things to do in a day

Fig. 1 (left). *The complete surround, with a feature panel – in this case a Delft tile – in place . If desired, this bottom part of the surround can be left out of the design.*

This clock surround has been made so that a feature panel can be incorporated just below the movement, as shown in Fig. 1. But this is not essential. If you wish to have a plain, square surround, you can easily adjust the dimensions shown.

Basic construction

If you do decide to make the surround as shown here, the feature on the panel will depend on the location of the clock. In this example, a Delft ceramic tile has been used to make an elegant living or dining room clock. But you may decide that the feature panel could contain a children's transfer (for a rumpus room), a cork plaque for a study, a copper motif for a kitchen – the choice is limited only by your imagination.

The choice of lumber is yours, too. Teak has been used here, but you could use mahogany or any similar hardwood. In fact, you could complete your project even more cheaply by using a softwood and staining or painting it.

The components are very simple and easy to make – in essence, just a base panel ("D") surrounded by a frame "E" and "F") with mitered corners, and three square cover panels ("A", "B" and "C") to conceal the clock movement.

Cut all wood as described in the cutting list, then glue "B" to "C", taking care to center one piece on the other, and glue these two panels to "D".

When all three panels are firmly fixed, screw them together from the back of "D", using two screws only on diagonal corners of a 4in (100mm) square.

Fitting the clock

Take the measurements of the clock movement and, using drill and coping saw or jigsaw, cut a cavity through "B", "C" and "D" panels for the clock movement to fit into.

The backplate of the clock will be larger than the actual movement, and this backplate can then be screwed on to the back of "D" to hold the entire clock firmly in place.

The final step in this stage is attaching the front panel "A". Drill a hole in the center of "A" just large enough to take the spline for the clock hands (the spline is the rod that turns the hands). Slip "A" over the spline and glue to "B", then fix "A" to the other panels by screwing through the other two diagonal corners of the 4in square on the back of "D".

Constructing the frame

The four borders "E" and "F" must first be mitered and to achieve perfect jointing you will need a miter box. These are available ready-made from hardware shops, but you can make your own quite easily with three pieces of lumber, forming the bottom and two opposite sides of a box.

A clock conversion

Once in a while you will dispose of a clock that keeps good time but which has become battered and worn, and no longer retains its youthful good looks. Next time this occurs, don't throw it away – with this interesting one-day project you can use the clock movement and transform your old, unattractive timepiece into a decorative feature for living room, dining room, bedroom, study or hall. In less than one day, your ancient clock will take on a whole new lease of life.

Using a try-square and rule, mark out a 45° angle from one side of the box to the other. With a tenon saw, cut both sides of the box at a 45° angle, and your miter box is complete, with a guide channel for future miters. Put a piece of the border lumber on its edge, into the miter box. Position and C-clamp it carefully so that one end of the border piece lines up with the 45° slot on the far side of the miter box.

Using a tenon saw guided by the 45° slots, cut through the border then reverse it in the miter box and cut the other end. Repeat this with the other three border pieces, making sure the miters are being cut right way around. Ensure, too, that your tenon saw has very sharp teeth, otherwise the miter joints will not fit well. Carefully smooth the mitered corners with sandpaper and glue the borders one at a time to "D", fixing them with small, slim nails.

Decoration

For the clock-face numbers, use transfer lettering such as Letraset, or cutout numbers from magazines – or even letter the numbers in

yourself. You may also feel that the original hands are unsuitable for your new clock – you could make up new ones from metal, wood or plastic.

Finally, if you've chosen to have a bottom front panel, attach the feature – ceramic tile, cork, copper, transfer or whatever. The feature should preferably be centered in the panel.

Finishing

If you've used teak, lightly rub teak oil into all surfaces. A more resilient finish with a teak-oil look can be created using 50/50 clear polyurethane varnish and mineral spirits. Apply one coat, brushing along the grain, and let dry. Sand down with fine sandpaper and apply another coat. Finish with very fine wire wool (Grade 000 or 4/0) and a light coat of teak oil. You now have an attractive yet practical

Fig. 2. *An angled cut-away view showing the panel sections, and with the clock in place.*
Fig. 3. *Side-section view, showing the various construction dimensions.*

feature, that has been made from something you would normally throw away.

Cutting list

Hardwood	Standard	Metric
A	$4\frac{1}{2}$ x $4\frac{1}{2}$	114 x 114
B	$5\frac{3}{4}$ x $5\frac{3}{4}$	146 x 146
C	7 x 7	178 x 178
D	$15\frac{1}{4}$ x $8\frac{3}{4}$	394 x 221

Depth of wood used in the above parts will depend on the depth of the clock you are using. Total depth of all four pieces when stacked together should be just a little less than the depth of the clock, from spline to backplate.

E (two off)	$15\frac{3}{4}$ x 2 x $\frac{1}{4}$	407 x 50 x 6
F (two off)	$8\frac{3}{4}$ x 2 x $\frac{1}{4}$	221 x 50 x 6

All standard measurements are in inches, and all metric measurements are in millimeters.

You will also need: Clock with appropriate fixing screws. Four screws to link "A", "B", "C" and "D". Wood adhesive. Two dozen slim nails. Decorative feature for bottom front panel.

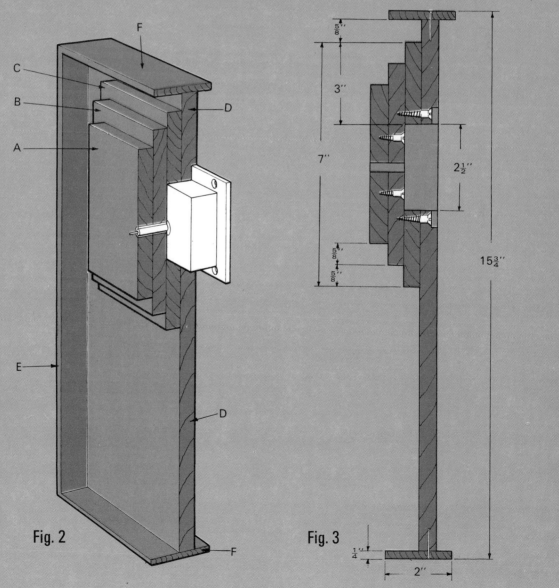

Fig. 2

Fig. 3

TRI-ART

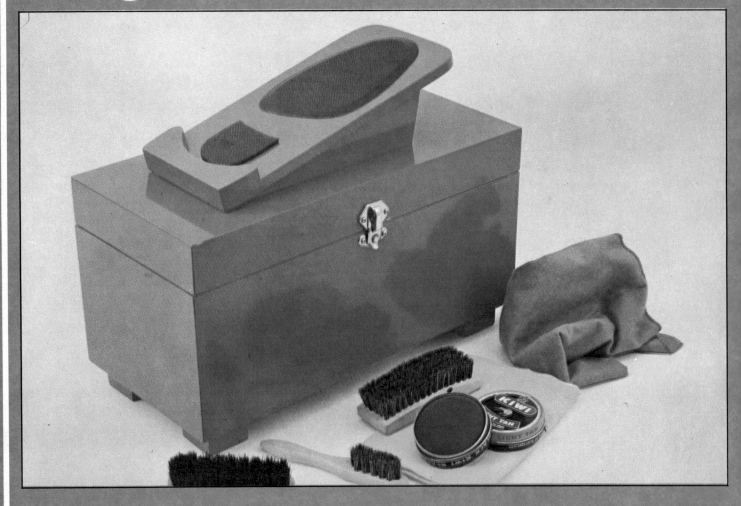

Custom-made shoe box

A professional looking shoe box is a really useful item which well repays the time spent on making it. This neat design holds all your brushes and polishes in an ample box. A footrest is built into the lid which allows you to polish shoes with the minimum amount of trouble and mess. The whole unit is strongly made and finished to give a lifetime's useful service.

Above. *This attractive and serviceable unit can be constructed with only the most basic of carpentry skills, and can, of course, be decorated to taste.*

Construction is quite simple provided you have measured and cut correctly. A wide range of woods, including plywood, is suitable for use. Your choice of material should be dictated by the functional purpose of the box – there is no need to use expensive hardwoods.

Measuring and cutting

Carefully mark out and cut the pieces to the sizes given in the cutting list. Some panels are cut so that they fit together in lapped joints as shown in the diagram. These joints give much stronger corners than the simple butt joint and are easy to make.

Begin with the base panel and mark a line around it ½in (13mm) from each edge. With a rebating plane cut a groove ½in (13mm) wide and ⁵⁄₁₆in (7·5mm) deep around the panel. The large lid panel is cut in exactly the same way. Now take the small side panels for the lid and the box and make identical rebate housings along the length of their shorter sides. The larger front and back panels are not rebated but simply slot into the grooves making a lapped joint. When the joints are cut, trial assemble to check for fit, then cut out the pieces for the footrest.

Cutting the footrest

The triangular pieces on which the footrest lies can be cut from a single piece of wood. First, mark a line diagonally from the bottom left-hand corner to the top right-hand corner. Then mark a point ½in (13mm) from the top left-hand corner. Repeat the process on the bottom edge measuring ½in (13mm) from the bottom right-hand corner. Draw lines from these two points to the tops of their respective triangles and cut the pieces out.

The actual footrest is ½in (13mm) wider at the top than at the bottom and is cut accordingly. The top corners are rounded off with a jig saw. The heelstop is cut to accommodate the shape of a heel and to lie flush with the edges of the footrest. The diagram gives you a guide to the shape of the heel stop and you can easily cut your own with a jig saw. Or a straight batten without a curve would do.

When all the pieces are cut to size sand them smooth with fine sandpaper.

Assembling the box

Begin by fixing the feet to the bottom panel. These are positioned at each corner ½in (13mm) from the edges. Use glue to fix them in position, and secure them with two ¾in (20mm) screws per foot.

Glue the front and back panels into the lapped joints on the side panels, making sure all the edges are flush. If there are any overlaps these must be sanded down before the bottom panel is added. Secure the panels with ¾in (20mm) slim nails. The bottom panel should drop neatly into position between the sides. If it overlaps at any point it can be planed and sanded down later.

Assembling the lid

First assemble the footrest unit by gluing and nailing the footrest proper to the triangular side pieces so that the long edges of the footrest overlap the side pieces by $\frac{1}{2}$in (13mm) and the narrow edge of the footrest lies flush with the narrow ends of the side pieces. Add the heel-stop by gluing and nailing, making sure it is flush with the edges of the footrest. Fix the unit to the lid so that it is positioned $2\frac{1}{2}$in (64mm) from one short edge, 4in (103mm) from the other short edge, and $1\frac{3}{4}$in (43mm) from the parallel long edge. Use three $1\frac{1}{4}$in (32mm) screws to fix each side piece to the top of the lid. The rest of the lid is assembled in exactly the same way as the box.

Finishing off

Fix 2in (52mm) brass butt hinges to the back panels of box and lid. They are housed in grooves cut to accommodate the thickness of the hinges and are positioned 2in (51mm) from each side of the box. A light brass chain 11in (280mm) is fixed by screws between the lid and the box. Finally, a snap catch is screwed to the front panels at their middle point.

Sand the box smooth to make the joints inconspicuous and fill any gaps with wood filler. When you paint the unit use an undercoat and at least two coats of good quality polyurethane gloss. To prevent wear on the footrest, stick a rubber sole and heel on it to give lasting protection to the paintwork.

Cutting list

Softwood A.P.A.	Inches	Millimeters
Bottom panel	$16\frac{1}{4}$ x $7\frac{7}{8}$	413 x 200
Top panel	$16\frac{1}{4}$ x $7\frac{7}{8}$	413 x 200
2 sides	$7\frac{7}{8}$ x $1\frac{5}{8}$	200 x 42
2 sides	$15\frac{7}{8}$ x $1\frac{5}{8}$	404 x 42
2 sides	$15\frac{7}{8}$ x $5\frac{5}{8}$	404 x 143
2 sides	$7\frac{7}{8}$ x $5\frac{5}{8}$	200 x 143
For the footrest		
1 piece	$9\frac{3}{4}$ x $2\frac{1}{2}$	248 x 64
1 piece	12 x $5\frac{1}{2}$	305 x 140
1 piece	$5\frac{1}{4}$ x 2	134 x 51

You will also need:
Wood adhesive
90 $\frac{3}{4}$in (20mm) slim nails (approximate)
14 1in (25mm) screws
2 hinges and 1 snap catch
A rubber heel and sole with glue
Tenon saw, rebating plane, hammer, block plane, sandpaper.
Paint.

Right. *An exploded view of the shoe box, showing the assembly of all major components. Further modifications, such as a partition inside the box, can be included by simply gluing panels in place.*

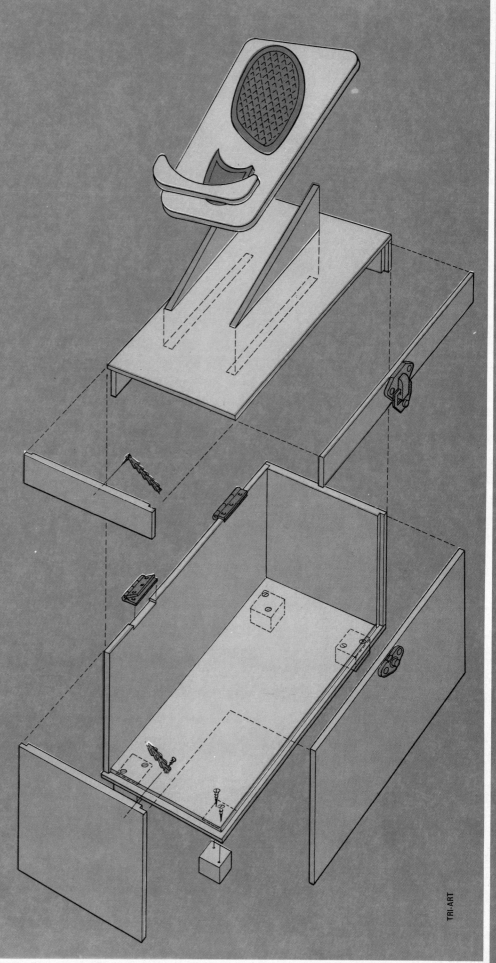

TRI-ART

things to do in a day

No adhesives, nails or screws are used to hold the box together. As shown in Fig. 3, protruding portions are cut out of the panels, and these are fitted into slots cut in joining panels – a simplified form of mortise and tenon joint – and held in position with split dowelling tapped trough holes cut in the 'tenons'. Use only marine or exterior grade plywood for the panels.

Cutting out

First cut the four sides, as detailed in Figs. 1-2, with the panel saw. Carefully mark out the outlines of the tenon portions and slots, then cut these out.

The tenons can be cut out with a tenon saw for the right-angled cuts from the outside edges, then the pad or coping saw for the parallel cuts. But if you have a powered jig saw, use this and the job can be done in a fraction of the time.

To cut the slots, first drill a $\frac{3}{4}$in (18mm) diameter hole at each end of the marked slot. Then cut through from each hole to the other along the cutside edges, with the coping or jig saw, to form the slot.

When the slots have been cut, briefly assemble the four sides to check that they fit properly. At the same time, take the opportunity of marking out the holes for the dowelling Dismantle the sides and cut the dowel holes with the brace and bit. Note that only half of each dowel hole must be visible when the box is finally put together.

Mark out and cut the base panel. Using the procedure outlined above, cut and shape the tenon projections. When you have done this, trial assemble the unit again to check for fit.

Finishing off

Next, round or bevel the sharp edges of all protruding tenon pieces. This is done with the bevel edge chisel. Carefully pare off the corners with the chisel, taking very small strokes – if you take off too much at once, you will have to fill the indentation, wasting valuable time. When the edges are well rounded, sand down to a smooth finish with fine sandpaper. If you prefer, the rounding off can be done with a toothed plane or file such as a Surfdom, but you will still have to finish off with sandpaper.

Now drill a series of drainage holes in the base panel, as shown in Fig. 4. Each hole is approximately $1\frac{1}{8}$in (28mm) in diameter. The size of the holes is not critical, but they must be distributed evenly over the panel.

The dowelling pieces are now cut into wedge-shaped halves, about $3\frac{1}{2}$in (89mm) in length. This is done by placing each one in a wood vise, upright and cutting downward, at a slight angle, with the tenon saw. As each pair of 'plugs' are cut, trial assemble the appropriate panels and fit the plugs in place by hand. When

Slot-together planter

This planter is not only attractive, it also has a rather unusual construction that provides many interesting and useful features. It is simple to make, and with a little imagination you could easily adapt it for other uses by altering the dimensions and using plywood of a different thickness. The main advantage of using this type of construction is that you can take the box apart for easy storage when it is not in use.

Above, left. *This attractive planter can be dismantled and packed away when not in use. This is because of its construction, which requires no glue, screws or nails – the panels are slotted together and secured with pegs fashioned from dowelling.*

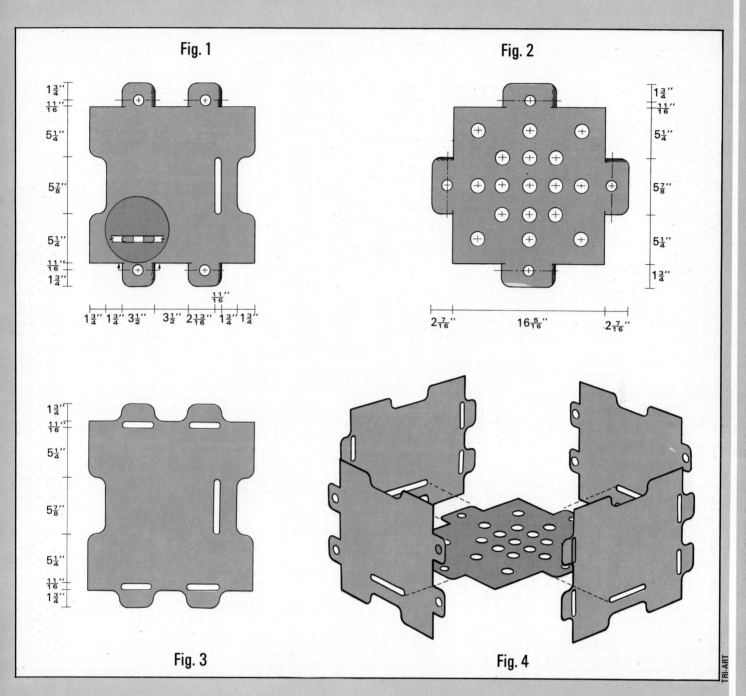

Fig. 1

$1\frac{3}{4}''$
$1\frac{1}{16}''$
$5\frac{1}{4}''$
$5\frac{7}{8}''$
$5\frac{1}{4}''$
$1\frac{1}{16}''$
$1\frac{3}{4}''$

$\frac{11}{16}''$

$1\frac{3}{4}''$ $1\frac{3}{4}''$ $3\frac{1}{2}''$ $3\frac{1}{2}''$ $2\frac{13}{16}''$ $1\frac{3}{4}''$ $1\frac{3}{4}''$

Fig. 2

$1\frac{3}{4}''$
$1\frac{1}{16}''$
$5\frac{1}{4}''$
$5\frac{7}{8}''$
$5\frac{1}{4}''$
$1\frac{3}{4}''$

$2\frac{7}{16}''$ $16\frac{5}{16}''$ $2\frac{7}{16}''$

Fig. 3

$1\frac{3}{4}''$
$1\frac{1}{16}''$
$5\frac{1}{4}''$
$5\frac{7}{8}''$
$5\frac{1}{4}''$
$1\frac{1}{16}''$
$1\frac{3}{4}''$

Fig. 4

TRI-ART

Fig. 1. *This is one of the side panels – the one that has the mortise holes cut along the 'corner' edges. The slot at the bottom takes the tenon of the base panel.*

Fig. 2. *This joins the panel shown in Fig. 1. It has tenon projections along the sides, and these slot into the mortises cut out of the adjacent panel.*

Fig. 3. *An exploded view showing the construction of the planter. The whole unit slots together. When cutting the panels, it is important to mark out by direct measuring and to constantly check the fit by trial assembly as each part is cut. This is particularly important for the dowel holes.*

Fig. 4. *Plan of the base panel.*

all the plugs are in place, tap them securely into place with the mallet.

The final step is a coat of protective paint or varnish. Because *marine or exterior grade* plywood is used, it is not necessary to apply more than one coat to weatherproof the unit. Although the planter has been designed for use in the garden, this should not be an excuse to leave a poor finish on the visible surfaces of the side panels; so sandpaper all visible surfaces down to a smooth finish before you apply a thick coat of paint or varnish.

This design will also make an excellent toy box for children. The only alteration to the design is to leave out the drainage holes, and use thinner plywood. With a little ingenuity, you could incorporate a lid and make an attractive chest.

Cutting list

Plywood	Standard	Metric
4 sides	$21\frac{1}{2}$ x 18 x $\frac{3}{4}$	539 x 458 x 18
1 base	$21\frac{1}{2}$ x $21\frac{1}{2}$ x $\frac{3}{4}$	539 x 539 x 18
Dowelling (or broom handle)		
12 pieces	$1\frac{1}{4}$ diameter	32 diameter

You will also need:
Fine-toothed panel saw.
Brace and bit.
Tenon saw.
Pad, coping or powered jig saw.
$1\frac{1}{2}$in, bevel-edge chisel, or toothed plane such as a Surform.
Small mallet.
All standard measurements are in inches. All metric measurements are in millimeters.

Handy shelf unit

This very attractive shelf unit is simply constructed of hardboard and wood. It can be used either freestanding or as a wall-hanging unit. Several units in a row will create a very unusual effect in a room decorated in a traditional style. The unit can easily be made in a day; in fact, the experienced worker can make several units in this space of time.

The method of using hardboard is particularly interesting. Two sheets of this material are used for the curved outside frame. These sheets are laminated together with a contact adhesive for maximum strength. As the sheets are glued together by their very 'rough' sides, the resulting material is a very strong hardboard, smooth on both sides.

Construction

Mark out, and cut, all the parts described in the cutting list. Cut the two upper shelves slightly oversize, and mark and cut to the final length using direct marking when the body has been built.

Mark out and drill the screw holes for the bottom shelf at each end of one panel of hard-

Above. A shelf unit that will add an attractive touch to any wall or alcove. It is the perfect place to display plants and ornaments and it will suit any room.

board. Using a try square, make sure that the bottom shelf is absolutely square. Stand the hardboard on end, and butt the *smooth* side to the end grain of the shelf. Secure the hardboard to the shelf with two screws.

When this has been done, *gently* bend the hardboard into an arch and screw the other end to the opposite end of the shelf. The hardboard is now in a 'U' shape, joined at the bottom by the shelf.

Using direct marking, hold the top shelf in the approximate position it will finally take, and mark out the positions for the ends of the shelf. Measure and cut the shelf, using the same method, and also the reinforcing batten.

Mark and drill the screw holes to take the

reinforcing batten along the rear top surface of the shelf. Butt the two members together and screw them together.

Drill the screw holes in the hardboard to take the top shelf. Screw this shelf into place, using a level if possible to check that the shelf is definitely level.

Finally, drill the screw holes for the middle shelf and fit this. The middle shelf is left until the end because the act of fitting the top and bottom shelves 'straightens' the sides, allowing the middle section to be fitted more easily.

Laminating the hardboard

Cut the second sheet of hardboard so that it fits over the curved first sheet exactly. Try this for size by bending it over the top of the unit.

When the fit is perfect, drill one screw hole in the middle of each end so that it can be fitted to the ends of the bottom shelf.

Spread contact adhesive over the rough surfaces of both hardboard panels. Stand the loose panel on end, locate the screw hole with one end of this bottom shelf, as described above (making sure that the rough, adhesive-covered surfaces will be brought together). When the adhesive has set according to the manufacturer's instructions, screw this end in place and carefully bend the hardboard into place as shown. Screw the opposite end in place.

Finishing

It is almost certain that the edges of the two hardboard panels will not flush exactly. If so, you will have to plane them down with either a plane set to fine, or one of the special toothed planes, such as the Surform, which have been produced for really smooth work.

Sandpaper all surfaces down to a smooth finish. If there are any fine gaps between the laminated hardboard, fill these with a cellulose filler used for wood and when dry sand down.

The unit can be finished with virtually any paint or emulsion. Or you could paint the hardboard and either leave the shelves natural, by giving them a coat of clear varnish, or cover them with Con-tact paper.

Cutting list

Wood	Standard	Metric
3 shelves	$18 \times 5 \times \frac{1}{2}$	$457 \times 127 \times 13$
1 reinforcing member	$18 \times 2\frac{1}{2} \times \frac{1}{2}$	$457 \times 64 \times 13$
Hardboard		
1 inner shell	$65 \times 5 \times \frac{1}{8}$	$1647 \times 127 \times 3$
1 outer shell	$65 \times 5 \times \frac{1}{8}$	$1647 \times 127 \times 3$

All standard measurements in inches, and all metric measurements in millimeters and meters. You will also require: Contact adhesive; at least 24 No. 4 1in (25mm) screws; paint, varnish or Con-tact paper.

Right. *The dimensions of the shelf unit and the positions of the components. The outer carcase is made of two sheets of hardboard glued together and bent into a curved shape.*

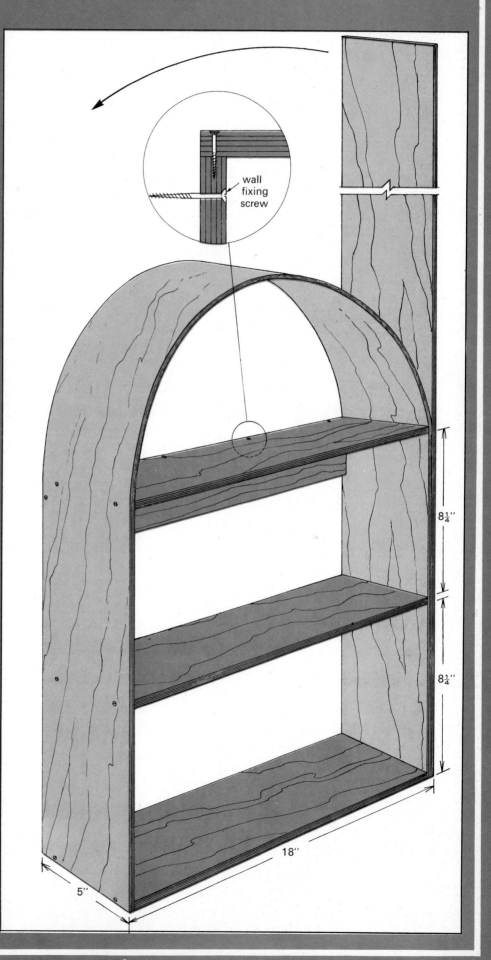

wall fixing screw

$8\frac{1}{4}''$

$8\frac{1}{4}''$

18''

5''

Kitchen hang-up unit

With just one day's work – and a little preplanning – you can make this attractive hang-up unit for your kitchen. All those small items which must be close at hand, but which clutter up the working surfaces given half a chance, are kept neat and yet convenient. And with its imaginatvely-designed and brightly-painted storage boxes, the unit will add that individual touch to your kitchen.

A place for everything. Storage boxes that hang on this custom-built unit make for an organised kitchen – and the idea could be adapted for use in other rooms.

Hanging things up in this way is such a good idea that you may find yourself thinking of a second unit for the hallway to hold both plants and flowers, or one to tidy up that home 'office' or workshop. The bathroom, too, might benefit from somewhere to put all those toiletries and cosmetics without tucking them out of sight. All you need to do is to adapt size and finish.

Preplanning

Make sure that before you start you have everything you need. There is nothing more frustrating than to find you are missing one vital nail – after the stores close. So buy all the supplies you are going to need in advance.

Simple construction

The hanging unit is simple and straightforward to construct – all you need is a saw, a screwdriver, a hammer and commonsense. Obviously a little previous experience will ensure everything goes as smoothly as possible, but anyone could undertake this hanging unit as a first project.

The main frame

Begin with the main frame members. Cut these accurately to length. Sand and polish the ends of these pieces as they will be seen when the unit is hanging in position.

The next step is to mark out and cut the half-lap joints at each corner of the frame. You should make sure that you mark only where you intend to cut and nowhere else. Then direct mark where to cut by laying the frame members across each other.

After cutting the joints, dry assemble the frame and check it for squareness by measuring that the diagonals are equal.

Drill holes for three ½in or 13mm screws in the rear members at each corner of the frame (see Fig. 1). Using covered-head screws means there is no need to countersink these drill holes. Apply a thin coat of wood adhesive to the joint surfaces, screw the frame together, again checking that it is square, and allow the glue to set.

Hanging bars

Drill a hole at each end of every hanging bar for a 1in or 25mm wood screw. Then glue and screw the bars to the main frame (see Fig. 1). Make sure that the bars are parallel to the horizontal frame members and that they are evenly spaced. You can use the side fillets, although they are not yet glued into position, to line up the ends of the bars.

Spacing blocks and side fillets

Four blocks act as spacers to hold the unit slightly away from the wall so that the hooks for the hanging storage boxes can slip easily over the horizontal bars (see Fig. 1). Set the rear blocks inward at the same distance as the thickness of the side fillets. The blocks are held in place by gluing to the back of the main frame members.

If you are planning to screw the unit directly to the wall, drill holes right through frame and blocks for wall-fixing screws as in Fig. 1. If you want to hang it from right-angled hooks, drill holes vertically through the two top blocks and hold all the blocks in place with 2in or 50mm wood screws driven through from the front of the frame. The raised cups in this case make a decorative feature.

Glue the side fillets in place, securing them with fine nails hammered into the spacing blocks and the ends of the hanging bars. This holds the fillets secure.

Finishing the unit

Once the unit is fully assembled, you can apply the finish you have chosen. Wood stains are available that enable you to match a rustic look in your kitchen. Alternatively you may wish to paint it in a bright color that will enliven your kitchen – or match your decorative scheme if you are planning to use the unit elsewhere.

One point: Let the paint dry properly. Even though this is a thing to do in a day, don't let your enthusiasm lure you into trying to cut corners.

Fixing to the wall

The kitchen hang-up unit can be screwed directly to the wall if you prefer, but you must check the wall surface before you start. An alternative is to screw two right-angled hooks into the wall at the level you want the top spacing blocks. Vertical holes drilled through these blocks allow you to hang the frame on the hooks. The advantage of this method is that you can take the unit down easily for cleaning.

Making a storage box

You can use your own imagination when assembling the storage boxes – making them longer and shallower than the one we tell you how to construct here, or leaving the front off so that you can slide boxes and bottles on and off.

Each box consists of four sides, the bottom and the handle as shown in Fig. 2. Construct the four sides first. The dimensions in the cutting list are for a square box. If you want to make the cut-away box shown in the diagram saw off the two diagonal cuts for the sides and cut down the height of the front panel and the handle to match.

Drill suitable 'finger' holes through the handle and fit this to the front panel by gluing it and nailing from the 'inside'.

Dry assemble the sides around the base to check that the frame is square, then glue and nail the butt-jointed sides together. The base is set into (that is, between) the sides. Glue the edges of the bottom panel, fit it into the frame, and secure it with nails through the sides.

Bend two pieces of angle bracket to form two right-angles which fit closely over the hanging bars (see Fig. 2). Then screw the brackets to the back of the storage box.

Finally, paint it with a brightly-colored paint that will make a cheerful kitchen.

Cutting list

Softwood A.P.A.	Inches	Millimeters
2 horizontal members	$36 \times 2 \times \frac{3}{4}$	$914 \times 51 \times 19$
2 vertical members	$27 \times 3 \times \frac{3}{4}$	$686 \times 76 \times 19$
16 hanging bars	$34\frac{1}{4} \times 1 \times \frac{3}{4}$	$870 \times 25 \times 19$
4 rear spacing blocks	$2 \times 2 \times 2$	$51 \times 51 \times 51$
2 side fillets	$27 \times 2 \times \frac{1}{4}$	$686 \times 51 \times 19$
For each storage box:		
2 back and front	$5 \times 3 \times \frac{1}{4}$	$127 \times 76 \times 6$
1 bottom	$5 \times 2\frac{1}{2} \times \frac{1}{4}$	$127 \times 63 \times 6$
2 sides	$2\frac{1}{2} \times 3 \times \frac{1}{4}$	$63 \times 76 \times 6$
1 handle	$3 \times 1\frac{1}{2} \times \frac{1}{4}$	$76 \times 38 \times 6$

Also needed (approximate quantities):
36 1in or 25mm brass wood screws with raised cups.
12 ½in or 12mm wood screws with raised cups.
Hooks or screws for wall attachment.
For each box:
30 ¾in or 19mm fine nails and 2 thin brass 1in or 25mm angle brackets and 2 ¼in or 6mm brass screws.
Wood adhesive.
Paint and wood stain.

Fig. 1. *Construction of frame corner.*
Fig. 2. *Exploded view of construction of hanging storage box.*

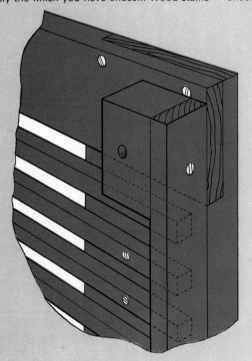

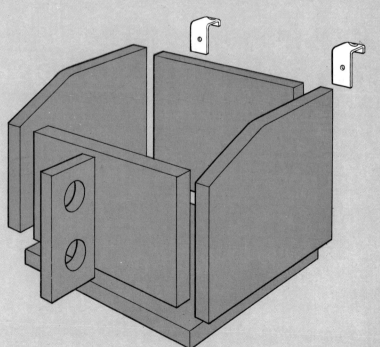

things to do in a day

NIGEL MESSETT

Hang-up pocket unit

If you've ever searched your kitchen in increasing frustration for the cooking utensil or cleaner that you had in your hand a moment ago, this hang-up pocket unit is for you. It gives you a place to store all those little items that so easily get lost and it also adds a splash of color to brighten your kitchen walls.

The hang-up pocket unit described here measures 33in x 24in (837mm x 610mm). It consists of a plain piece of backing fabric and four pockets which are sewn to the backing fabric. Each pocket is divided into four sections by vertical lines of stitching. A dowel at the top allows a length of cord to be attached so that the unit can be wall hung from a hook, and a dowel at the bottom gives sufficient weight for

Above. *Save yourself the frustration of 'losing' items in the kitchen. This hang-up pocket unit provides a handy storage place for a range of items and the attractive patterned fabric will brighten any wall.*

the unit to rest reasonably flat against the wall when filled.

Materials

To make the hang-up pocket unit to the dimensions shown here you will need:
—¾yd plain denim, 36in wide, for the backing material.
—¾yd patterned fabric, 36in wide, for the pockets.
—10ft of ¼in elastic for gathering the pockets.
—a 26in length of ⅝in diameter dowel for the

hanging pocket unit.
—a 24in length of ⅝in dowel for the bottom of the unit.
—a length of cord and a wall-fixing hook to hang the unit.

The backing material

The backing for the pocket unit is made from a piece of ¾yd plain denim, 36in wide. A non-patterned material, like that shown in the photograph, goes attractively with the floral-patterned material used for the pockets.
To make up the backing material, first check that the edges of the fabric are square with the grain. Then make a 1in wide hem along the raw 27in edges of the backing material. To do this, turn in under ½in onto the wrong side and then turn under another 1in. Machine stitch the hems. Now make the casings for the dowels at the top and bottom of the backing material. Turn under the selvages onto the wrong side for 1½in. Machine stitch along the edge.

The pockets

To make the pockets, first divide the patterned fabric into four equal strips. Then turn under and press down a ½in fold along the bottom long edge of each strip. Along the top edges, turn under ¼in onto the wrong side and press down. Fold under another ½in and machine stitch along the fold. Now make another line of machining along the outer fold of each hem — this helps the gathers form attractively when the elastic is inserted.

Placing the pockets

Divide and mark the short side of the backing material into quarters. Do this with the long side of each pocket strip also. Place the pocket strip, long side down, onto the right side of the backing material. Position the pockets so that they are equally spaced and the marks correspond.

Attaching the pockets

Now take the 10ft length of ¼in elastic and divide it in four. Insert one piece into each casing at the top of the pocket strips and draw up to fit the backing material loosely. Turn under ½in along each short end of the pocket strips and pin to the backing material so that the fold is ¼in from the edge.
Pleat the bottom edge of the pockets to fit each section and tack in position. Machine stitch the sides and bottom edge of the pockets to the backing material. Take the stitching over the ends of the elastic to secure it. Divide the pockets into sections by stitching from top to bottom at each quarter mark.

The dowels

Insert the longer length of dowel into the casing at the top of the backing material so that 1in extends on each side. Put the shorter length into the casing at the bottom and stitch up the end of the casing to hold the dowel in position.

Hanging the unit

An ordinary picture hook is quite adequate for hanging the unit — it is not heavy when filled. To attach a length of cord to the top dowel, drill a small hole in the top dowel, close to each end. Take a piece of cord of suitable length and thickness, tie a knot near one end and thread the other through one of the holes in the dowel. Thread the cord through the other hole and tie a knot. Trim off the excess cord, knock the picture hook into the wall and hang the pocket unit.

Other locations

You can, of course, use the pocket unit in rooms other than the kitchen — you will find many good uses for it in the home. In the living room, for example, it can form a clever place to store your sewing and knitting materials — though you should keep your knitting needles in a safer place, out of the reach of young children. In your bedroom, next to the dressing table, the pocket unit can be used for cosmetic bottles and aerosols while, in a child's room, it can be the ideal place for soft toys and small books. Use the unit in your hallway and you need never search the house for your favorite head scarf or pair of gloves again.

Below. *You can vary the design of pocket units to suit your needs. Some of the pockets in this example, which is made of plastic-coated cotton edged with tape, have been made large enough to accommodate quite bulky items.*

Design variation

Pocket units are very versatile around the home — and you don't have to make them in fabric. One useful design incorporates a backing sheet of hardboard with cardboard boxes glued onto it — providing receptacles for pens, pencils, writing paper, envelopes — in fact, anything that will fit in the boxes.

Square sectioned boxes can be made by simply folding flat pieces of cardboard to the required shape. Semicircular boxes can be cut from cardboard tubes — the sort posters are mailed in are ideal — with cardboard added to form the bottom of the receptacle. A couple of applications of spray paint, in the color of your choice, will give you a good looking and useful storage unit.

things to do in a day

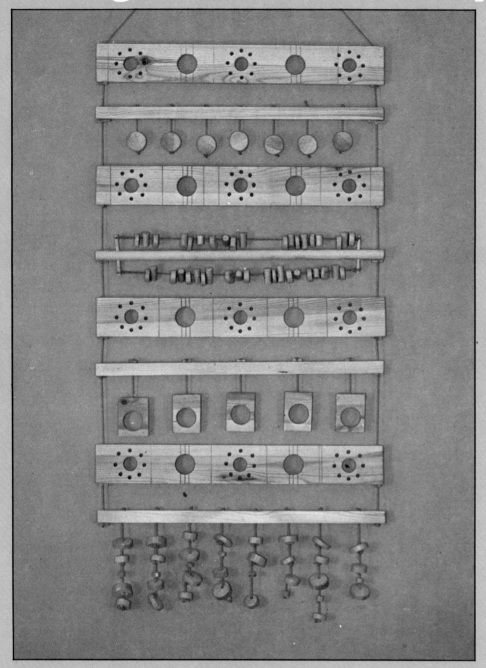

Create a fun thing

If you have a blank expanse of wall space you wish to make more interesting, or a corner that could show a mobile off to good effect, here is something a little different, and extremely cheap and simple to make. By scaling up the design a most distinctive room divider can be produced, again with ease, in the space of one day.

All the material required is a selection of pine – or any other wood that appeals to you – off-cuts or even scraps, a few assorted dowels, and some strong colored twine. With only a minimum of carpentry skills, the project will take

less than a day, and whatever finish you decide on can be applied in a little extra time.

Design aspects

The basic design as shown in Fig. 1 is no more

than a skeleton for you to hang your own ideas on. For example, a different layout of the drilled holes, or a different shape of hole, variation of the sizes of wood used, or the overall size, can all be employed according to taste. More suspended elements might be included if you are thinking of a mobile as the final result. Two small beaten copper dishes fixed to either end of one of the lower boards could be used to hold candles or incense sticks.

The finish you apply depends, of course, on how and where the design is being used. A natural, austere look is perhaps best served by two light coats of matte polyurethane varnish over the normal grain of the wood. Alternatively, a variety of bright, glossy colors might be called for to suit your particular decor.

Construction and tools

For a typical wall-hanging, 3in x ¾in (75mm x 19mm) and 1in x ½in (25mm x 13mm) offcuts and assorted dowels are required. In this project there are three diameters of dowel used – thick dowel of a diameter around 1in (25mm) for the circular sections hanging from the second cross-board, this and ½in (13mm) diameter sections hanging from the last cross-board, and small diameter dowel pieces for the stops at the base of the threading holes.

The tools that are essential for this job are a brace, a tenon saw, and a selection of bits – these will depend on what design of holes you decide on, and what type and thickness of wood you are working with. The large holes can be drilled with either a center bit, or, better still, a Forstener bit. These, however, are more expensive than the center bit, and are not as readily available. A vise, or a bench hook, is a very useful addition to this short list, but is not an absolute necessity. A vee-block (see Fig. 2) will be a decided help in cutting whatever dowel sections you are going to include in your own version of the design.

The actual construction consists of three main stages: the drilling of the frontal decorative holes and of the vertical side holes through which the threading twine passes, the cutting of circular dowel sections and the making of any other ornamental pieces you think will blend in with your design (see, for example, the string of dowel 'beads' in Fig. 1), and the final assembly using the twine.

In the first part, uniformity of position of the holes can be obtained, and considerable labor saved, by clamping boards together with C-clamps and drilling the frontal holes right through all of them at the same time. For this, however, you will need a Jennings bit (a type of auger bit), in place of the center or Forstener bit mentioned above (see Fig. 3).

A helpful trick to keep in mind when you are cutting the dowel sections is to wrap a piece of paper around the dowel and use this as a guide for straight, parallel cutting (see the dowel length in Fig. 2).

Once the wood has been prepared, there is very little more to do. Make sure that the threading holes are wide enough to allow the twine good clearance. On the other hand, they should not be so wide that smooth and straight drilling through the wood is made difficult, as the drill is passing through a narrow but long section of the board. This means, of course, that the drill does not have to wander too far off its line for it to break out onto the visible surface. There is a way of avoiding this problem entirely, but it is up to you to decide whether or not it clashes with the rough and natural aspect of the design too much to fit in with your concept of the finished product. Small curtain wire hooks are screwed into place where the threading holes enter and leave the board. The twine, or small-linked strong chain, is then connected to top and bottom in pieces, rather than having one continuous length threading each hole in turn.

An attractive room divider, or a partition to mark off an area into sub-sections, can be made along the same lines as above, scaling up width and height as appropriate. The result is surprisingly substantial, and will successfully visually break up, say, a large living and sleeping area. Some provision must be made for the increased weight of the enlarged structure. This can be done by threading with two lengths of twine instead of the usual one, and/or by suspending from two points in the ceiling.

Whatever purpose you have in mind for this, you must be careful when threading the parts together to get them level. The cross-boards are kept in place, and immediately supported by, small pieces of dowel knotted into the twine across the threading holes (see Fig. 1). A small groove, cut with a knife around the center of the dowel piece, will help to keep the knot in place. You can either level as you go by sliding the knot into the exact position required, or measure up the twine in advance. In this case, mark in where the knots are to be tied and, since the ends are always free as you work down, it is an easy matter to include the dowel stops as you come to them.

You have more or less total freedom in a project of this kind to adapt your ideas to chime in with the use you are going to put it to. The restrictions placed on you by the materials involved are so minimal that you can change around almost all the details and suggestions given above and still come out with a worthwhile addition to the interior of any suitable room.

Fig. 1. *The unit is best threaded with one twine length; some decorative ideas are shown.*
Fig. 2. *A vee-block can be used to keep the dowel stable during cutting. The paper strip, taped in place, ensures a straight cut.*
Fig. 3. *Use C-clamps to drill up to four boards together. A piece of scrap is placed between each clamp screw and the top board to distribute pressure and prevent wood marking, another large piece underneath to guide the bit cleanly through the exit of the last hole.*

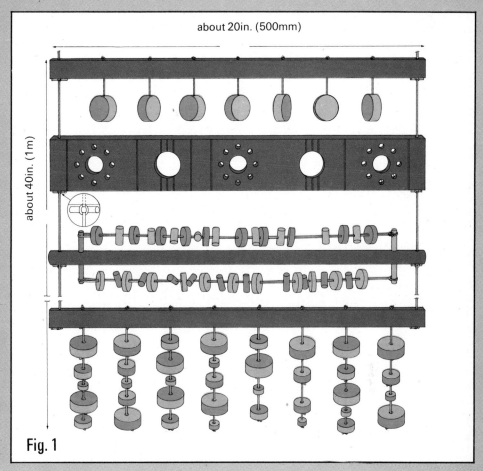

about 20in. (500mm)

about 40in. (1m)

Fig. 1

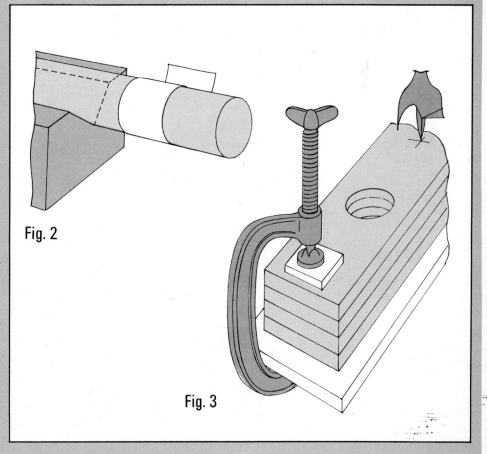

Fig. 2

Fig. 3

A bathroom cabinet

This neat and simply constructed bathroom cabinet gives you plenty of space for the large range of cosmetics and toiletries that your family collects.

Modern houses often have small, box-like bathrooms with little space to store the range of cosmetics and toiletries which your family accumulates. This wall-hung bathroom cabinet solves that problem, giving you ample storage space. The cabinet is also hard-wearing and attractive and so simple to make that you can easily do the job in a day.

The cabinet is made from ½in (13mm) plywood which is covered with plastic laminate. There are two shelves, the lower one running the length of the cabinet and the upper one running about half the way across the cabinet. The front of this shelf, at the end in the middle of the cabinet, is curved. The front edges of the shelves are set back 1in (25mm) from the front edge of the cabinet.

The cabinet doors run on two ½in (13mm) wide plastic runners. At the top of the cabinet the runner is butted to the underside of the top component. At the bottom the runner is set into a rabbetted groove so that it is flush with the inner face of the bottom component. The back of the cabinet is hardboard that is nailed and screwed in place. The only joints used in the construction are butted and screwed. The doors can be replaced with specially cut mirror

glass if you require a reflective surface in this position, or you can use ordinary glass doors.

The cabinet sides

The first step is to cut the sides, top and bottom of the cabinet to the sizes given in the cutting list. Mark out the boards with each pair of components laid together. Cut the boards a little overlong and plane the ends square. Clamp a piece of waste wood to the end which you will plane – this prevents damage to the corner of the boards.

When you have cut the components, glue plastic laminate to the inside face of the two side pieces. If you try to apply the laminate here after all the assembly has been carried out you will have to make awkward cutouts around the shelves or have unsightly joins between two pieces of laminate.

Cut the laminate to size and spread a contact adhesive over the reverse side and the inside face of the sides. Let the glue go tacky and then lay the laminate on the boards. Place weights – a few books will do – on the laminate and allow the glue to dry.

The next step is to cut the rabbet on the front facing edge of the cabinet bottom. This allows the plastic runner for the doors to be glued in place flush with the inside face of the bottom piece. The rabbet is ½in (13mm) wide and 5/16in (8mm) deep. Cut the rabbet right along the board with a rabbet plane.

The sides, top and bottom of the cabinet can now be assembled. The ends of the top and bottom components butt the ends of the inside faces of the sides. The sides are fixed to the top and bottom with three 1¼in No. 6 countersunk screws at each corner. Spearielist screws are best for this job – they are designed specifically for man-made boards and have greater holding power than ordinary screws. Position the screws about 1in (13mm) inward from the long edge of the boards and one in the center. Drill the holes in the sides first and, using these as a guide, mark the position of the holes in the end grain. Drill all the holes and countersink the ones in the sides. Screw one side to the top and bottom and check that the angle is square. Then screw the other components together and measure the diagonals of the box to check that it is square. Plane the corners flush if necessary.

Glue laminate on the inside faces of the top and bottom pieces. The plastic strips that are the door runners can now be glued in place. The lower runner fits into the rabbet in the bottom piece, the top runner butts the front inside face of the top piece. The top runner is deeper than the bottom runner – this allows you to put the doors in place easily.

The cabinet back

The back of the cabinet is made of hardboard. The rough side of this is covered with plastic laminate. Cut the hardboard to the size given in the cutting list and make sure it is square. Glue a piece of laminate to it. Lay the back panel on the box construction with the laminate downwards and fix it to the back edge of the cabinet components with $\frac{1}{2}$ in slim nails.

The long shelf

Cut the lumber for both shelves to the sizes given in the cutting list. The lower shelf runs the whole length of the cabinet and is positioned $6\frac{7}{8}$ in (174mm) up from the inside face of the bottom piece. Mark this distance on the inside face of the two sides.

Before you fit the shelf, cover it with plastic laminate. Cover the top and bottom faces first and then apply a strip of laminate to the front edge. The laminate used as edging strip is half the thickness of the laminate used for the faces of the components. Always apply edging strip last – this makes the joins between the pieces of laminate a little less conspicuous.

Lay the box construction on its back on a flat surface. Put the shelf in place with its bottom edge on the two points you have marked. Draw round the outline of the shelf edge on the inside of the box with a soft pencil. Drill two holes between these lines through the sides from the inside of the box. With the shelf held in place, use a sharp pointed tool such as a bradawl and push it through the holes in the sides to mark the positions of the holes on the ends of the shelf. Drill the holes and screw the shelf in place with $1\frac{1}{2}$ in No. 6 countersunk screws. Secure the shelf further with slim nails, knocked through the hardboard back into the back long edge of the shelf.

The short shelf

This is $12\frac{3}{4}$ in (324mm) long and ends about halfway across the length of the box. This end of the shelf is curved, the curve having a radius of $2\frac{1}{4}$ in (57mm).

The shelf was cut to length earlier. To form the curve, measure $2\frac{1}{4}$ in (57mm) along the long edge and $2\frac{1}{4}$ in along the short edge from one corner. The point where these lines intersect is the center of the circumference. With a compass, mark the curve on the board. Cut this out with a coping saw and finish the curve with a spokeshave.

Cover the top and bottom faces with laminate. Then apply edging strip to the edge that has the curve. The edging strip is half the usual thickness of plastic laminate so it will bend around the curve quite easily.

The doors

Each door is made from three sheets of laminate glued together. Cut them to the exact size given in the cutting list – don't make them smaller or bigger or they won't fit. Glue the three laminate pieces for each door together.

When the glue has dried fit handles to the door. The type of handle you use is up to you but brass colored handles look good against the laminate used on this cabinet.

Finishing

Apply laminate to the outer faces of the sides, top and bottom. Trim up the laminate where necessary with a small smoothing plane. Apply edging strip to the facing edge of the cabinet's outer components. The edging strip is butted at the corners.

Before you hang the cabinet, coat the reverse side of the back panel with varnish. This 'balances' the laminate on the other side and prevents the hardboard from warping. Drill four holes in the back of the cabinet and drill and plug your bathroom walls. Fix the cabinet in place with $1\frac{1}{2}$ in No. 8 countersunk screws.

Cutting list

Plywood	Standard	Metric
2 sides	$18 \times 6 \times \frac{1}{2}$	$457 \times 152 \times 13$
top & bottom	$24 \times 6 \times \frac{1}{2}$	$610 \times 152 \times 13$
1 long shelf	$22\frac{15}{16} \times 5 \times \frac{1}{2}$	$583 \times 127 \times 13$
1 short shelf	$12\frac{3}{4} \times 5 \times \frac{1}{2}$	$324 \times 127 \times 13$
Hardboard		
1 back panel	$24 \times 18 \times \frac{1}{8}$	$610 \times 457 \times 3$
Plastic laminate		
6 pieces for doors		
(3 for each)	$16\frac{7}{8} \times 11 \times \frac{3}{32}$	$429 \times 279 \times 2.35$
for rest of		
cabinet	13 sq ft	1.21 sq m
edging strip	11ft	3.35m

All standard measurements are in inches and all metric measurements in millimeters, except where stated.

You will also need some $1\frac{1}{2}$ in No. 8 countersunk screws, some $1\frac{1}{4}$ in No. 6 countersunk screws, some slim nails and contact adhesive.

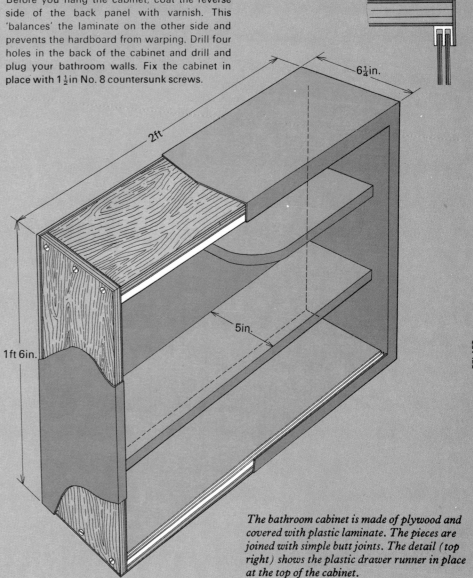

The bathroom cabinet is made of plywood and covered with plastic laminate. The pieces are joined with simple butt joints. The detail (top right) shows the plastic drawer runner in place at the top of the cabinet.

Fitting a false ceiling over a bath gives a neat and attractive appearance to the shower curtain. You can choose the color of the curtain to match your decorative scheme.

Preplanning

As with all day-long projects a certain amount of preplanning is necessary. In this case, it consists of choosing and buying the curtain fabric and curtain track, and buying and preparing the wood.

The curtain fabric must be waterproof and heavy enough to hang properly. Nylon fabrics are available in a wide range of patterns and colors – so wide that selection may be the problem, rather than finding one to match the decorative scheme in your bathroom. You can very easily spend an evening in advance to make up the curtains. Alternatively, if you are sharing the labor one of you can sew the curtain while the other erects a false ceiling. You must remember to use the correct tension on your sewing machine when you are working with heavy plastic materials.

Purchase the curtain track at the same time that you buy your material. There are plenty available in the stores. In this case you must fit an all-plastic track to ensure that you have no problems with metal corrosion.

The amount of wood you need to buy depends on the length of the false ceiling you plan to erect and on the width of your bath. Once you have measured these dimensions you can calculate the length of the battens, and the amount of tongued and grooved pine boarding you require.

This unit consists of a framework of 2in x 1in and 3in x 1in battening attached to the walls on three sides. The front is covered with a 9in x 1in plank, which acts as a fascia, covering the curtain rod and to a certain extent providing extra bracing. The underside of the frame is lined with 6in x $\frac{3}{4}$in T & G pine boarding – although other woods would do just as well.

Preparation of lumber

Because of the location of the unit, there will always be a certain amount of moisture in the wood – unlike, for example, woodwork in a living room. Because of this, all wood used should be given at least two coats of a good wood weatherproofing preservative. This prevents deterioration of the wood or the growth of fungus. But make sure that the preservative used will enable you to use varnish or paint on the wood afterwards. Your dealer will explain which types are best.

Construction

First, using direct marking, cut the side and rear members that will butt against the ceiling. These are shown in Fig. 1. When the lengths are correct, cut the halving joints. The short cross members are halved at each end (remember to allow for the extra width of the 3in batten at the front), and the long rear one at each end and for a T-halving in the middle.

Now screw the rear and side members to the

Roof-in your shower

When you fit a shower to a bath, whether as a permanent wall-mounted fixture or as a removable attachment, a shower curtain is essential – without one, water goes all over the floor. Putting in a false ceiling together with its own fascia board to conceal the shower curtain fixtures will give a new look to your bathroom – and lowering the ceiling height above the bath gives a stylish coziness to having a shower.

Take a look at your bathroom and see just what a difference this 'thing to do in a day' could make and how it would fit in. Our photograph and diagrams show a bath which fits exactly along one wall of a bathroom. If your bathroom is wider than the length of the bath you can run the false ceiling across the full width of the room while stopping the curtain track short, or even bending it around to carry the curtain across the end of the bath.

Extending the false ceiling in this way preserves a major advantage of our design: The weight is carried by the walls. As a result of this you will not encounter the kind of difficulties that can occur when trying to suspend a structure by screwing it into the ceiling joists. The construction is quite simple and easy to carry out step by step.

wall, making sure that you have achieved a good firm grip. All screws used in this type of construction should be stainless steel or brass to prevent corrosion problems.

Repeat this procedure with the bottom frame, leaving a 2in or 50mm gap between the top and bottom frames. You may find at this stage that walls and ceiling are slightly out of true. Direct marking of this lower frame allows you to fit it exactly.

Using direct marking again, cut the top front member – which is the 3in x 1in length that lays across the recess in the short cross members – and the middle member of the top frame. Briefly dry assemble these to check for fit. Repeat this with the long front and middle members of the lower frame, dry assembling to check to fit.

Mark and cut the fascia, then screw the top front member to it at 3in intervals, with screws through the front of the fascia, as shown in Fig. 2. This right-angled section can now be eased into position as shown in Fig. 1, and secured by two screws at each end through the underside of the end battens. Now ease the middle cross member into place. This is

secured in the same way at the front, and is glued and skew-nailed to the rear member at the back.

With the fascia in position, cut and fit the front and middle members of the lower frame. In this case the screws at the front pass through the short battens first and into the long member. Next screw the front member of the lower frame to the fascia from the inside, at 3in intervals.

The frame and fascia are now in position. Measure, cut and fit the T & G boarding underneath. This is secured with slim nails, the heads of which are sunk with a nail punch. Don't use screws to secure the T & G because the slim nails allow for a certain amount of expansion and contraction. If a gap shows between the boarding and the wall at the rear, this can be covered with wooden coving.

The fascia will have a certain number of holes where screws have been countersunk. Fill these recesses with grouting filler and when dry sand down.

The unit is now ready for a coat of varnish over the T & G, and a coat of paint over the fascia. As with the fabric, you can match the paint to your decorative scheme – virtually all modern paints

can stand up to the damp conditions of a bathroom.

When the paint and varnish are touch-dry, you can fit the curtain rod in place. The final stage is to hang the shower curtain from the track. With a heavy plastic curtain, eyelets let into the top hem can provide a simple and strong way of suspending the curtain from the hooks.

Cutting list

Solid wood	Standard	Metric
3 long members	2 x 1	50 x 15
1 long member (top front)	3 x 1	75 x 25
6 short cross members	2 x 1	50 x 25
Fascia	9 x 1	229 x 25
T & G boarding	6 x ¾	152 x 19

All standard measurements in inches; all metric measurements in millimeters. The lengths of members and fascia and the quantity of T & G boarding will depend on the length and width of the bath.

Also required: Curtain rod (and curtain). 1¾in stainless steel or brass screws. 1½in copper slim nails. Wall-fixing screws and plugs.

Fig. 1. *The false ceiling is constructed from battening and T & G boarding with a fascia board that carries the curtain rod out of sight. You will need to measure your own bathroom to plan the dimensions for your construction.*
Fig. 2. *A detail of the fascia attachment shows fixing screws driven through from the front. These holes can be filled before painting.*
Fig. 3. *An end view shows the length that you must allow for the curtain.*

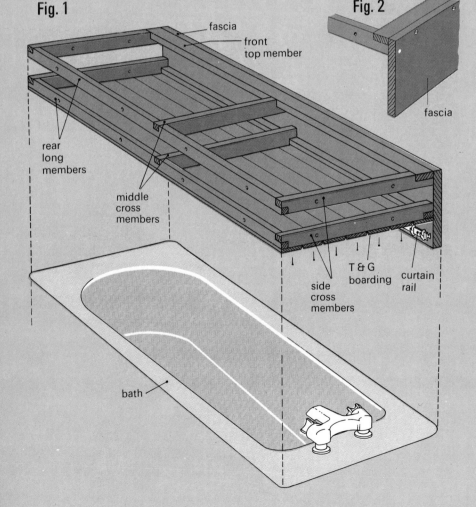

Fig. 1

fascia
front top member
rear long members
middle cross members
side cross members
T & G boarding
curtain rail
bath

Fig. 2

fascia

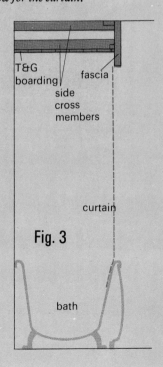

T&G boarding
fascia
side cross members
curtain
bath

Fig. 3

A space-saving folding table

Foldaway tables have long been a favorite carpentry exercise for the average home handyman: With their particular combination of compact utility and simplicity of construction, it is not difficult to understand why. The kitchen, the children's bedrooms and the den are all candidates for the installation of a foldaway table or desk — in fact, any room that needs an extra working surface, perhaps only from time to time, may be nicely complemented by the addition of one.

By scaling the design up or down you can adapt the foldaway to your specific situation and requirements. Within the limits of the materials and construction techniques used, you have quite a good deal of scope to change not only the size but also the concept of the finished article. Various suggestions in this respect are included in a later section of this chapter.

Materials and accessories

The foldaway essentially consists of three rectangular pieces of plywood, joined together with piano hinges and a drop-flap stay. The piece fixed to the wall is further provided with stripping, which can be made from off-cuts of the plywood, so that the whole table will fold back into a compact, visually neat wall hanging. You will also need four 2in (50mm) No. 6 screws and a selection of small nails. The former are to fix the back piece to the wall, but if you have some other method of fixing in mind you will not require them. The nails are for attaching the stripping (see Fig. 2) to the sides of the wall piece — remember that (if you think there is any danger of splitting the plywood as you drive them through the stripping) slightly blunted nails may be called for.

The drop-flap stay, as shown in Fig. 1, should have an arm-length of around 3½in (88mm). It is quite possible that the stay, as supplied, will be made so that the screw attachments at either end are facing in opposite directions, which is not suitable here. In this case, you simply take out the rivet at one end and turn the attachment to face in the same direction as the other.

The catch at the top that holds the folded table

in can be made in many ways — the pattern shown in Fig. 2 is a very simple type, but is just as effective as a more elaborate hook-and-eye clasp, or something along the lines of a spring-loaded catch fitted to the top stripping.

The foldaway can be finished in paint, varnish, or even covered with a fabric that will harmonize with the room it is built for. Since the leg flap is going to be visible whenever the table is in the folded position, it is obviously this surface that should receive the most attention when the decorative angle is considered. The finish naturally depends on how the end product is to be used — for example, if it is to go in a youngster's room, a dartboard, perhaps backed by a corkboard sheeting as a protection for the wood, could be screwed into the leg flap. Alternatively, a thin blackboard surface can be

fixed to this flat, to serve either as a daily bulletin board if the table is, say, used as an ironing board/general extra kitchen working surface, or just for doodling if it is in a child's room. Another idea that might appeal is to inlay (or paint) a chessboard on the table flap.

Construction and cutting

A piece of standard ⅜in (9mm) plywood, measuring 3ft x 8ft (0·9m x 2·4m), is a suitable size for the type of table described here, but clearly this depends on the size of table you have in mind. A foldaway ironing board will, for example, be narrower and longer, whereas a foldaway kitchen table will probably need to be about the same length but a little wider. Within reason, the dimensions can be quite drastically changed around, the main point to watch out for being the relative size of the pieces — that is, allowing just the right amount of clearance between the pieces when they are folded up. Too little will either result in pressure at the top catch or even make it impossible to close the table up properly, while too much will be unsightly.

With this in mind, therefore, the following pieces can be cut:

wall – 24in x 31½in or 600mm x 775mm desk top – 23¾in x 30¾in or 594mm x 769mm leg (support) flap – 23¾in x 30in or 594mm x 750mm.

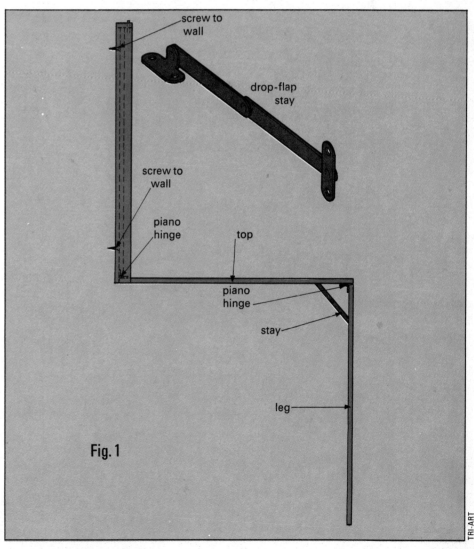

Fig. 1

Labels on figure: screw to wall; drop-flap stay; screw to wall; piano hinge; top; piano hinge; stay; leg

TRI-ART

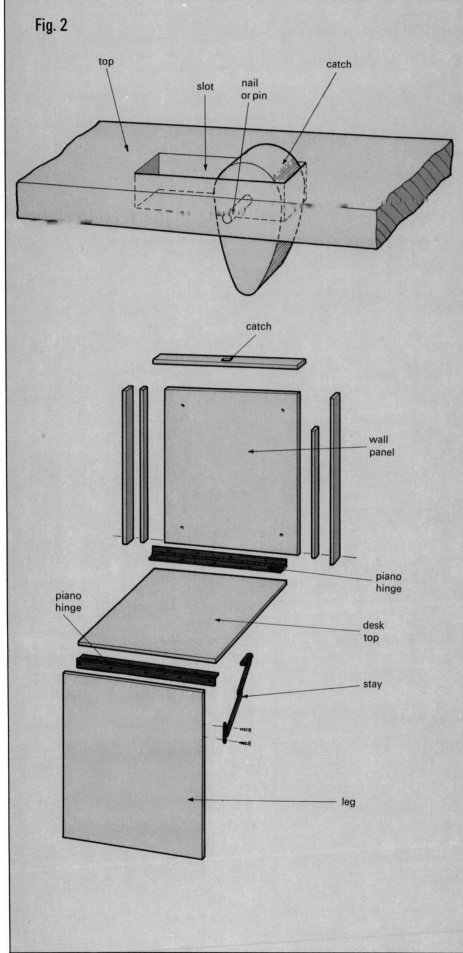

Fig. 2

top

slot

nail
or pin

catch

catch

wall
panel

piano
hinge

piano
hinge

desk
top

stay

leg

Three lengths of stripping, $1\frac{3}{4}$in (44mm) wide, are then cut from the plywood board. Two of them should be long enough to fit flush with the two vertical sides of the wall piece, with the other cut to meet these two at the top corners in whatever joint you decide on. In the table shown on p.62, no joint has been used at the corners, and if the finished product is to be more functional than decorative, this might appeal to you also. On the other hand, if you want a more decorative effect, a box or comb joint is certainly most suitable of the worked joints for this type and size of wood. You may, of course, decide on simply running the ends of the stripping together and then glue and nail them, using dovetailed nailing.

The back edges of the stripping are fitted flush to the back of the wall piece and tacked into place with $\frac{5}{8}$in (16mm) slim nails or tacks. The vertical sides of the wall piece must be fitted with additional stripping (see Fig. 2), around $\frac{3}{4}$in (19mm) wide, to take the main stripping out clear of the folding pieces. Remember that this subsidiary stripping must be cut short on the side where the drop-flap stay is fitted, and be sure to fix the stay so that it folds up neatly along the side of the two flaps it connects.

A detail of the top piece of stripping with its clasp for the folded flaps is shown in Fig. 2. The idea and its execution are both elementary, and yet provided the carpentry has been done carefully and the folded flaps are not under any abnormal pressure to pop out, it is quite effective. Once the three main pieces have been measured and cut, they are joined with the piano hinges, which are themselves tailored to fit from end to end of the edges they join. With the flaps in the folded position, the stripping can now be added, but make sure there is adequate clearance before actually finishing the tacking on. It is probably safest to put the top stripping in loosely before making the slot and tongue catch, so that the slot can be positioned just in front of, or level with, the 'front' (i.e. the bottom, when in use) of the flap that serves as the table surface. The slot itself can either be gouged out with a handyman's knife, or drilled and then chiseled out. The tongue, which is just a small piece of wood (preferably with the ends rounded) must be cut to pivot around through 180°.

To fix the finished article to the wall, a masonry drill should be used to insert the fiber or plastic plugs that take the screws. This part of the job requires meticulous attention, since the stability of the table depends largely on the accuracy with which the wall piece has been positioned. After the screws have been securely fixed, the facing for the wall piece can be glued on. The wall piece of the table shown here has been fronted with corkboard, but this again is entirely up to you.

Fig. 2. *Exploded view of the complete construction. On the desk shown on page 62 the edge battening does not joint or butt. This is purely for decorative effect. If the unit is to be used a lot, it would be better to join the corners. Gluing and nailing is the simplest method, but for a really secure join make a box, or comb, joint.*

TRI-ART